# Alcibiades

# Alcibiades

Walter M. Ellis

**Routledge**
London and New York

First published 1989
by Routledge
11 New Fetter Lane, London EC4P 4EE
29 West 35th Street, New York, NY 10001

Typeset by Columns of Reading
Printed in Great Britain by T.J. Press (Padstow Ltd). Padstow, Cornwall

*British Library Cataloguing in Publication Data*

Ellis, Walter M., *1943–*
Alcibiades. — (Classical lives).
1. Greece. Politics. Alcibiades,
ca. 450-404 B.C.
I. Title   II. Series
938'.04'0924

ISBN 0-415-00993-6
ISBN 0-415-00994-4 Pbk

*Library of Congress Cataloging in Publication Data*

Ellis, Walter M., 1943-
Alcibiades/Walter M. Ellis.
p.    cm. — (Classical lives)
Bibliography: p.
Includes index.
ISBN 0-415-00993-6. ISBN 0-415-00994-4 (pbk.)
1. Alcibiades. 2. Greece–History–Peloponnesian War, 431–404
B.C. 3. Statesmen–Greece–Biography. 4. Generals–Greece–Biography.
I. Title   II. Series.
DF230.A4E44 1989
938' .05'0924–dc19
[B]

To my wife, Sue

# Contents

Table of figures     x

Abbreviations and short titles     xi

Acknowledgements     xiii

Preface     xiv

1 **Family, youth, and early influences**     1

2 **Alcibiades and the early stages of the Peloponnesian War**     24

3 **Alcibiades and the peace of Nicias, 421–416**     36

4 **Sicily and defection**     53

5 **Recall, triumph, and death**     69

Appendix: Alcibiades, Genos, and Eupatridae     99

Chronological table     103

Notes     104

Select bibliography     133

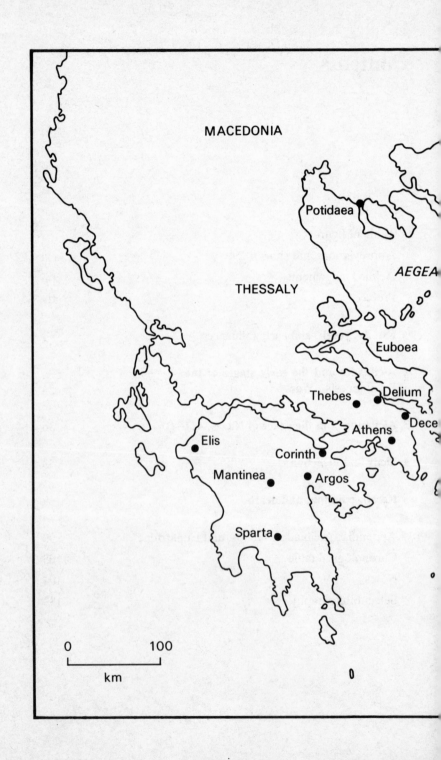

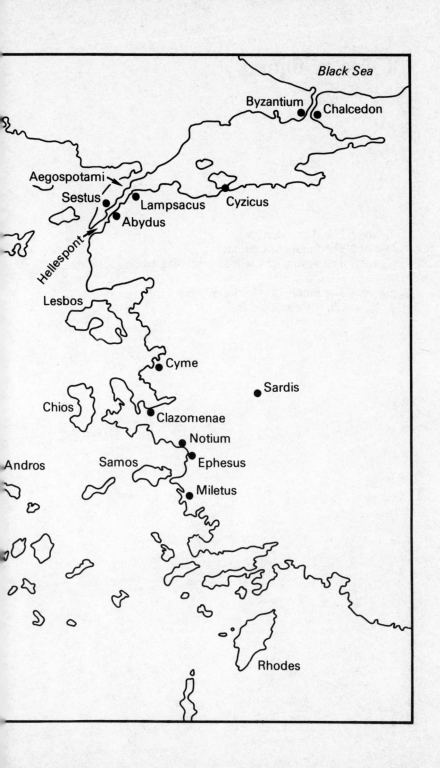

# Table of figures

*Figure 1* The Alcmaeonids                                    2
*Figure 2* The family of Cleinias                             6
*Figure 3* The family of Cleinias according to
             other scholars                                   7
*Figure 4* The family of Alcibiades' wife                    32
             Chronological table                            103

# Abbreviations and short titles

| | |
|---|---|
| *AFD* | B.D. Meritt, *Athenian Financial Documents of the Fifth Century* (Ann Arbor 1932) |
| *AJAH* | *American Journal of Ancient History* |
| *AJP* | *American Journal of Philology* |
| *ATL* | B.D. Meritt, H.T. Wade-Gery, and M.F. McGregor, *The Athenian Tribute Lists*, 4 vols: I (Cambridge, Mass. 1939), II–IV (Princeton, NJ 1949–53) |
| *BCH* | *Bulletin de Correspondance Hellénique* |
| Beloch | K.J. Beloch, *Griechische Geschichte*, 2nd edn (Strassburg and Berlin 1912–27) |
| *BSA* | *The Annual of the British School at Athens* |
| Bury–Meiggs | J.B. Bury, *A History of Greece*, 4th edn, revised by R. Meiggs (London 1975) |
| Busolt | G. Busolt, *Griechische Geschichte* (Gotha 1893–1904) |
| *CAH* | J.B. Bury, S.A. Cook, and F.E. Adcock (eds) *Cambridge Ancient History*, vol. 5 (Cambridge 1927) |
| *CP* | *Classical Philology* |
| *CQ* | *Classical Quarterly* |
| *CR* | *Classical Review* |
| Davies, *APF* | J.K. Davies, *Athenian Propertied Families 600–300 BC* (Oxford 1971) |
| *FGrH* | F. Jacoby, *Die Fragmente der griechischen* |

| | |
|---|---|
| | *Historiker*, 3 vols: I–II (Berlin 1923–6), III (Leiden 1940–58) |
| *GG* | *Griechische Geschichte* |
| Grote | G.Grote, *A History of Greece* (London 1888) |
| *HAC* | C. Hignett, *A History of the Athenian Constitution* (Oxford 1952) |
| Hatzfeld | Jean Hatzfeld, *Alcibiade* (Paris 1951) |
| *HCT* | A.W. Gomme, A. Andrewes, and K.J. Dover, *A Historical Commentary on Thucydides*, 5 vols (Oxford 1945–81) |
| *IG* I³ | David Lewis (ed.) *Inscriptiones Graecae* (Berlin 1981) |
| *JHS* | *The Journal of Hellenic Studies* |
| Kagan, *Peace of Nicias* | D. Kagan, *The Peace of Nicias and the Sicilian Expedition* (Ithaca, NY and London 1981) |
| *LSJ* | H.G. Liddell, R. Scott, and H.S. Jones, *Greek–English Lexicon* (Oxford 1940) |
| *ML* | R. Meiggs and D. Lewis, *A Selection of Greek Historical Inscriptions* (Oxford 1969) |
| *MPhL* | *Museum Philologum Londiniense* |
| *OCD²* | N.G.L. Hammond and H.H. Scullard (eds) *The Oxford Classical Dictionary*, 2nd edn (Oxford 1970) |
| *PCPS* | *Proceedings of the Cambridge Philological Society* |
| *RE* | A. Pauly, G. Wissowa, and W. Kroll, *Real-Encyclopädie der Classischen Altertumswissenschaft* |
| *REG* | *Revue des études grecques* |
| *RhM* | *Rheinisches Museum für Philologie* |
| *TAPA* | *Transactions of the American Philological Association* |
| Wade-Gery | H.T. Wade-Gery, *Essays in Greek History* (Oxford 1958) |
| *ZPE* | *Zeitschrift für Papyrologie und Epigraphik* |

# Acknowledgements

Mortimer H. Chambers has taught me almost everything I know about the Athenian empire, Greek epigraphy, and the critical reading of ancient sources. I thank him for his efforts, his persistence and his patience. I began to write about Alcibiades in my second quarter at UCLA in a seminar taught by Jack Cargill. I would like to thank him and those other teachers who have been especially helpful: Ronald Mellor, Steven Lattimore, and Charles D. Hamilton. My graduate colleagues Geraldine Moyle, Lester Field, and especially Ralph Gallucci have been a great help to me. I would like to thank Geneva Phillips for her understanding, and my brother Charles Ellis and my aunt Mildred Bainbridge for their love and support. Most importantly, I owe a special debt to my wife, Sue Ellis, without whom this book would never have been written.

# Preface

> I am enamoured of two things, Alcibiades, son of Cleinias, and philosophy.
>
> Socrates, a paraphrase from the *Gorgias* (418 d)

Alcibiades inspired passionate reactions from his contemporaries, and, indeed, he has continued to inspire them down through the ages. Few figures in ancient history come to life so vividly as does this charming schemer in the pages of Thucydides, Plato, and Plutarch. Plutarch (*Alc.* 1.3) reminds us that, although we do not even know the names of the mothers of the prominent generals who were Alcibiades' contemporaries, tradition has preserved for us the names of Alcibiades' nurse and his tutor.

Modern historians tend to see Alcibiades as a representative of the decline of Athens in the late fifth century. They brand him an 'opportunist' with all the reproach they can muster and compare him unfavourably with the great Athenians of previous generations, such as Pericles and Themistocles. Alcibiades, indeed, did not look or behave as a politician should. He was very handsome, and he was known to have had many affairs with people of both sexes. He drank heavily and caroused through the streets of Athens at night associating with actors, musicians, and prostitutes. He was wild, reckless and extravagant, and as Thucydides (6.15) noted, he indulged his desires beyond his means.

Some of these very qualities, however, account for his popularity. Like Shakespeare's Henry V, Alcibiades had the common touch. He was intimate with people of every kind and learned to understand them in ways that his more cautious contemporaries, who associated primarily with their own class, could only guess at. The ancient historians were not harsh in their judgements on Alcibiades, considering the wildness of his character. Even the sober and slightly stuffy Plutarch admired his amiability and saw charm even in his moral lapses (*Comp. Alc. and Cor.* 3.4).

Any discussion of the ancient sources for the life of Alcibiades, however, must begin with Thucydides. Thucydides was not only Alcibiades' contemporary, but arguably the most brilliant, critical, and impartial historian of the ancient world. The biographer of Alcibiades is truly fortunate to have such a historian, rare in any age, as his guide and most important source. Thucydides strove to be impartial. He saw history, not in the caprices of individuals, but in the decisions of nations. These decisions for war and for peace were made by governments, sometimes wisely and sometimes foolishly, but always after debate and always as the collective will of a people. Thucydides showed that individuals can influence history, but it is the nation that adopts the individual's policy, and it is the nation that is ultimately responsible for the enactment of that policy. Thucydides does not inform the reader, for instance, whose arguments led to the massacre of the Melians (5.116.4); it was an Athenian decision, and that is all that mattered to him. He showed little interest in personality or in any other issue that was ancillary to his main goal, the history of the Peloponnesian War. He does not tell us moderns, in short, many of the details we would like to know. We have to go to other sources to learn many of the particulars of Alcibiades' life.

Thucydides' wall of impartiality broke down in some places. We know his attitude toward Pericles (highly favourable), for instance, and toward Cleon (unfavourable). As a personality, Thucydides spends more time on Alcibiades perhaps than on any other figure in his *History*, but his attitude toward him is difficult to discern. His most direct assessment of Alcibiades (6.15.3–4) states that he was an excellent military leader, but also that he was lawless and ambitious. Thucydides blames the people for turning away from him and choosing lesser men. He does not blame Alcibiades directly, but the reader is left with the impression that Thucydides believed that Alcibiades should have behaved more discreetly if only to avoid the contumely of the populace. Alcibiades dominates the eighth book of Thucydides' *History*. This book was left in an unfinished state, and it may be that its final form would have taken a very different shape. But, as it is, Alcibiades' presence in it has led some modern historians to suggest that he was a major informant for Thucydides. While this is a credible theory, the information does not seem to have prejudiced Thucydides' treatment of his informant in one direction or another. Modern historians find abundant ammunition in Thucydides to either praise or condemn Alcibiades. Thucydides' *History* ends abruptly while narrating the events of the year 411. For the remainder of Alcibiades' career, we must turn to decidedly inferior sources.

Although Xenophon is our best source for the end of the Peloponnesian War, he has always suffered in the inevitable comparison with Thucydides. He wrote a history, the *Hellenica*, that covered the Greek world from 411, from approximately where Thucydides left off, down to 362. He was born in Athens in the late fifth century and grew up during the Peloponnesian War. He left Athens in 401 and joined an army, which supported Cyrus the Younger's unsuccessful attempt to capture the throne of Persia. Xenophon narrated the events of this campaign in the *Anabasis*, his best-known and most admired work. He was exiled from Athens, took up service with Sparta and eventually came under the personal patronage of King Agesilaus. He lived most of the remainder of his life in the Peloponnese but may have returned to Athens after 366. Xenophon was an admirer of Socrates and wrote several works about him. He also wrote on a variety of other subjects from hunting to economics. The *Hellenica* is more like a personal memoir than the sort of detailed and objective history that Thucydides wrote. It has had its share of detractors. One recent review of the work summarized, 'his historical judgements were superficial, his interests narrow, and his omissions astounding even within the range of his interests' [George Cawkwell, 'Introduction', in *Xenophon: A History of My Times (Hellenica)* (Harmondsworth 1979) 16]. One of those astounding omissions was Xenophon's failure to mention anywhere the assassination of Alcibiades. His assessment of Alcibiades is not obvious but seems, on the whole, positive. Alcibiades always has a central role in Xenophon's description of the battles in which he took part. Xenophon gives two views of Alcibiades (*Hell.* 1.4.13–17). The positive view is full and laudatory, however, while the negative one is brief and cursory.

In order to balance Xenophon's inadequate handling of the end of the war, we must compare it to that of Diodorus. Diodorus of Sicily lived in the first century BC. He wrote a universal history from murky mythological beginnings down to his own time. Characteristically, he would borrow mainly from one source at a time, and it is generally agreed that Ephorus was his primary source for fifth-century Greece. Ephorus of Cyme was a historian of the fourth century BC, whose work, lost except for fragments, stretched from the return of the sons of Heracles down to his own time. Ephorus was a student of Isocrates, the famous teacher of oratory, and, as a historian, he was more interested in rhetoric and style than content. He did not have Xenophon's military knowledge, and his descriptions of battles are often stock pieces that are artificial and even reused in later centuries with slight variations. However, he was well read, and he consulted, among others, Ctesias, Hellanicus, Philistus, and the Oxyrhynchus historian. [See G.L. Barber, *The Historian Ephorus* (Cambridge 1935)]. Ephorus' original narrative was doubtless superior to the version we get in Diodorus, but neither historian was a match for Thucydides. It is only when we get to the year 411 that Diodorus can be of any use, and even here, he must be approached with caution. Diodorus can be a useful foil to Xenophon, however, and must not be dismissed automatically. His accounts of the battles of Cyzicus, Notium, and Aegospotami are especially helpful.

Plutarch's biography of Alcibiades provides us with many details that Thucydides did not think sufficiently important. Plutarch chose details that he believed would reveal his subject's character. In the first chapter of his *Alexander*, he states that his role as a biographer is to illuminate the virtues and vices of a man and not necessarily to tell of his great achievements. Plutarch wrote about Alcibiades at a distance of half a millennium. In assessing Plutarch's worth as a source, it is necessary to remember this distance, the author's purpose and his essential naïveté. However, Plutarch was well read and capable of critical thinking, and he had access to a great number of works that are lost to us. For his *Alcibiades* and the related *Nicias*, Plutarch utilized a wide range of sources including Thucydides, Aristophanes, Antiphon, Xenophon, Ephorus, Andocides, Isocrates, Hellanicus, Plato, and Duris of Samos. He also made use of Philistus of Syracuse (*c*.430–356 BC), one of the most important historians of the western Greeks in the classical era. Philistus was alive at the time of the Sicilian expedition, and he later served as an adviser to Dionysius I. His work covered Sicilian history from the earliest times down to and including the reigns of Dionysius I and Dionysius II. Philistus was admired by such later writers as Cicero and Quintilian, who compared him to Thucydides. Plutarch also consulted Theopompus, a student of Isocrates and contemporary of Ephorus. Like Ephorus, Theopompus was fond of rhetorical devices and often subordinated accuracy to style. Theopompus differed from Ephorus in his bias; the latter was an admirer of Athenian democracy, but Theopompus was not. Plutarch also alludes to Antisthenes, a follower of Socrates and founder of the Cynic school of philosophy, and Theophrastus,

Aristotle's successor. One has only to compare his life of Alcibiades with that of Nepos to see Plutarch's superiority in the art of biography. (Nepos' *Alcibiades* does have some useful information, however, especially concerning his subject's final days and death.) In addition to Plutarch's life of Alcibiades, the modern historian can find some useful details in his lives of Solon, Themistocles, Aristides, Pericles, Nicias, and Lysander.

A fragment of another biography of Alcibiades [B.P. Grenfell and A.S. Hunt (eds) *The Oxyrhynchus Papyri* (London 1903) III, no. 411, pp. 31–5] has been found. It covers briefly the mutilation of the herms and Alcibiades' defection to Sparta. The author has read Thucydides and probably Andocides, and the life seems to belong to the period of the early Roman Empire. It has little independent value and differs from other sources only in its rather generous assessment of Alcibiades' accomplishments in Sicily.

Perhaps the most indelible portrait of Alcibiades from antiquity has been given to us by Plato in the *Symposium*. Who can forget the drunken young general who shows up at Agathon's party, late and uninvited, and proceeds to pour forth his love of Socrates in a speech that is both touching and funny? As a close companion of Socrates, Alcibiades naturally makes several appearances in the dialogues of Plato. In addition to the *Symposium* and the passage from the *Gorgias* quoted at the beginning of this Preface, Alcibiades appears in the *Protagoras* and in two eponymous dialogues, the second of which is probably not by Plato. [For discussions of the genuineness of *I Alc.*, see A. Lesky, *A History of Greek Literature* (London 1966) 512.] Plato, of course, was a philosopher, and his concerns were philosophic. The dialogues were never meant to reproduce actual conversations. Still Plato's audience was not at a great distance from these events, and certain details may be legitimately accepted as historical.

Because of his colourful life, it is not surprising that Alcibiades was the source for many anecdotes in antiquity. He is often mentioned by such orators as Isocrates, Andocides, Lysias, Demosthenes, and Lycurgus. Isocrates, who wrote a speech in defence of Alcibiades' son, is the most informative but also the most frustrating. Isocrates' speech, *De Bigis*, has many inaccuracies and half-truths. Alcibiades was also a popular subject for such anecdotal writers as Aelian and Athenaeus. These writers cannot be ignored, but should be viewed with even greater scepticism than the orators.

The first modern, scholarly biography of Alcibiades was

*Alkibiades der Staatsmann und Feldherr* by G.F. Hertzberg
(Halle 1853). Hertzberg's work was substantial for its time, but it
failed to incorporate the significant body of late-fifth-century
inscriptions that have been collected and analysed over the years.
It was superseded in every way by the *Alcibiade* of Jean Hatzfeld,
published in 1940, and republished with minor revisions in 1951.
Hatzfeld's book is an admirable piece of scholarship and has been
a great help at every stage in the creation of this biography.
Forty-six years of scholarship have altered and increased our
knowledge of the late fifth century, but Hatzfeld's work is still
impressive. *Alcibiade* is more than a biography in the narrow
sense; it is, as its subtitle explains, a study of Athens in the late
fifth century. Hatzfeld was not afraid to take a stand, and, if his
interpretations sometimes place him in a minority of one, his
work is both thoughtful and lively. There has never been a
biography in English that could be favourably compared with
Hatzfeld's. E.F. Benson's *The Life of Alcibiades* (London 1928)
is not, by modern standards, a scholarly work. E.F. Bloedow's
eccentric thesis [*Alcibiades Reexamined, Historia* Einzelschriften Heft 21 (Wiesbaden 1973)] that Alcibiades had little
effect on history has won him few supporters. Alcibiades, with
the exception of Hatzfeld, has been better served by articles
and shorter works including those by J. Toepffer [*RE s.v.*
'Alkibiades', cols 1516–33], P.A. Brunt [*REG* 65 (1952) 59–96],
R.J. Littman [*TAPA* 101 (1970) 263–76], H. Bengtson [*Zu den
strategischen Konzeptionen des Alkibiades* (Munich 1979)], and
P.J. Rhodes ['What Alcibiades did or what happened to him'
(Durham 1985)]. E. Delebecque's full-length attempt [*Thucydide
et Alcibiade* (Aix-en-Provence 1965)] to prove that Alcibiades
was one of Thucydides' informants is not a significant improvement over Brunt's article, just cited.

Alcibiades sought to be an Athenian leader in the tradition of
Themistocles and Pericles. This was the consistent goal of his life.
It is true that his behaviour was eccentric and often self-
indulgent; it is also true that he was an opportunist, but this
admission should not blind us to his goals or his merits. Modern
historians have too often blamed Alcibiades for Athens' defeat in
the war and decline as a polis. Thucydides, our most important
source for the life of Alcibiades, did not make a scapegoat of
him, and neither should we. Thucydides (6.15.3–4) blamed the
Athenian people for turning to lesser leaders; however, it cannot
be denied that Thucydides had an ambivalent attitude toward
Alcibiades. On the one hand, he seems to hold him up as an
example of one of the inferior successors to Pericles, and, on the

other, he seems to decry Athens' failure to follow her best leader. It may be, as P.R. Pouncey says, that Thucydides intended to record the former view but was 'prompted by his sympathy for Alcibiades to shade it' toward the latter [*The Necessities of War* (New York 1980) 110]. However, it is also possible that Thucydides, as so often, was trying to make a very fine point. Athens was to blame for not trusting Alcibiades, and Alcibiades was to blame for causing that distrust. Athens condemned Alcibiades and sent him into exile. Alcibiades brought harm to Athens who, when she had suffered great losses, called him home to help her. Alcibiades returned to Athens and made great strides in reviving her prospects of winning the war, but she exiled him again because she could not trust him. The modern mind thinks in didactic terms. If only Athens could have trusted Alcibiades, she could have won the war and avoided disaster. If only Alcibiades could have behaved more moderately, the Athenians would have allowed him to remain in a position of leadership. But perhaps this is a misguided effort. The Greek mind, steeped as it was in fifth-century tragedy, could see a certain inevitability here and a certain symmetry. If Alcibiades had been more moderate, he would not have been Alcibiades. The Athenians had a moderate leader in Nicias, and this was part of the problem. If Athens had been more steadfast in her support of Alcibiades, she would not have been Athens. We might recall the words of the Corinthian ambassador to Sparta in Book I of Thucydides. They apply equally well to Athens and to Alcibiades.

> Athenian daring will outrun its own resources; they will take risks against their better judgment . . . Suppose they fail in some undertaking; they make good the loss immediately by setting their hopes in some other direction . . . In a word, they are by nature incapable of either living a quiet life themselves or of allowing anyone else to do so.
> [Thuc. 1.70. Trans. Rex Warner (Harmondsworth 1972) 76].

# Chapter one

# Family, youth, and early influences

Alcibiades was born in the middle of Athens' greatest century. We cannot be certain about the year of his birth, but the year 450 is a reasonable approximation.[1] This means that Alcibiades was a contemporary of many of Athens', indeed the ancient world's, most illustrious citizens. He knew many of them personally. His relationships with Pericles and Socrates are well documented, but Alcibiades would have been well acquainted with many of the other great men of his time. He could easily have known Sophocles, Phidias, Euripides, Thucydides, Aristophanes, Plato, and Xenophon. Athens, with a citizen population of about 40,000 was not a large city by modern standards.[2] But what is perhaps of greater significance is the fact that Alcibiades lived in a culture that was primarily oral. Everything from business to philosophy was transacted in dialogue. A man's place was in the boule or in the agora, but always in the company of others. Their word for a private man, *idiotes*, is our word for an idiot. Alcibiades was equipped in every way to rise to the top of this society. Although his speech was impaired by a lisp, he managed to turn even this liability into an asset. He used the lisp to render his speech more personal and more persuasive.[3] Whatever other assets Alcibiades may have had, his family connections were of the very best. He was descended from two of Athens' most prestigious families.

## The Alcmaeonids

On his mother's side Alcibiades was descended from the Alcmaeonids, perhaps the most influential family in the history of Athenian politics. The Alcmaeonids traced their ancestry back to Nestor, the king of Pylos and participant in the Trojan War.[4] The names Megacles and Alcmaeon appear in the list of Athenian life-archons,[5] but Megacles I, who lived in the late seventh century, is the first member of the family to emerge from the mists of legend into the realm of verifiable history. Megacles I ordered the deaths of the followers of Cylon (*c*.632) and thereby brought down a curse on his descendants. Cylon was a young aristocrat who tried to make himself the tyrant of Athens. He had won a victory at Olympia in 640[6] and had married the daughter of Theagenes, the tyrant of Megara. Thucydides tells us that Cylon's seizure of the Athenian acropolis was in an Olympic year.[7] The year 632 seems to be the most likely choice. A later date is possible, but by 632 Cylon would have had time to secure his alliance with Megara and to have readied his forces. The venture seems like a young man's enterprise, and the longer he waited, the dimmer the memory of his Olympic victory would have grown. Megacles I was archon for the year.[8] Thucydides tells us that when the Athenian people learned that Cylon had seized the acropolis, they came in from the country to resist him.[9] Cylon and his brother escaped, but the rest of his supporters were starved into surrender. They left the acropolis under the protection of the gods and with the understanding that their lives would be spared. Megacles I and the other archons had them massacred.

The family of Megacles I was tried for sacrilege.[10] Myron of Phlya was prosecutor, and the Alcmaeonids were found guilty.

## The Alcmaeonids

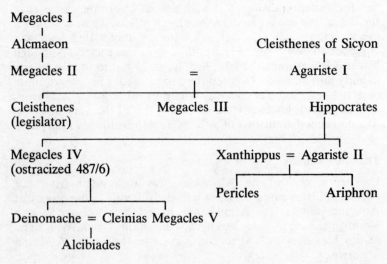

*Figure 1*

The members of the family who were still alive were banished, and the bodies of those who had died were cast out of their tombs and removed from Attica. Even after the accursed had gone, the pollution remained. Epimenides of Crete was summoned to purify the city. We cannot be certain when this trial and purification took place, but some time in the 580s is a reasonable supposition. The narrative order of Aristotle's *Constitution of the Athenians* suggests that these events occurred before the Draconian law code of *c*.621. Plutarch's *Solon* places these events at the time of Solon. The later date seems to be more likely because both versions emphasize that the guilty were dead and buried. This fact suggests that more than ten years had passed. We can assume that Megacles I was a fairly young man at the time of his archonship. It seems likely that the opposition to the massacre grew slowly, perhaps aided by the authorities at Delphi who had encouraged Cylon's attempted coup.[11] Megacles I was probably dead by the time of the trial, and the banishment was carried out, as Plutarch says, against the 'descendants' of Megacles.[12]

It is a tribute to the brilliance and industry of this family that they were able to overcome this crippling blow to their prestige. The curse cast a very long shadow. King Cleomenes of Sparta used it against Cleisthenes in the late sixth century at the very moment the great lawgiver was pursuing the reforms that would begin to turn Athens into a democracy. Two centuries after the archonship of Megacles I, the Spartans raised the issue again. One of the first actions taken by the Spartans after they voted for war against Athens in 432 was to send a demand to their adversary that they expel the curse from the city. This was an obvious attempt to undermine the authority of Pericles. Strictly speaking, neither Pericles nor Alcibiades were Alcmaeonids since they were related to this family through their mothers. But Spartan propaganda suggested that the curse was transferable from the mother to the son. The charge could have been brought at some time against Alcibiades. In him the curse came full circle. Like his distant ancestors, he too was tried and condemned for sacrilege. After him no member of his family, not even by maternal descent, is known to have been prominent in Athenian politics.

Alcmaeon, the son of Megacles I, received the family's fortune from the king of Lydia. Herodotus tells the amusing story of how he was invited to Sardis by Croesus and encouraged to take as much gold as he could carry at one time from Croesus' royal treasury.[13] Alcmaeon put on a baggy tunic and big boots. He filled them with the gold dust that he also sprinkled on his hair and stuffed into his mouth. Croesus was so amused at Alcmaeon's appearance that he gave him twice as much gold as he was carrying. Herodotus says that this was the source of the Alcmaeonids' wealth, and that Alcmaeon was able to keep racehorses that led to an Olympic victory.

There is overwhelming evidence to suggest that the chronology of this encounter is impossible. Alcmaeon led the Athenian contingent in the First Sacred War.[14] This war centred around the seige of Cirrha that ended in 591/590.[15] The war is generally thought to have begun about 595.[16] If Alcmaeon had been about thirty years of age at this time, he would have to have been about seventy by the time Croesus' envoys visited Delphi around the year 550. This is unlikely, but not impossible. But Herodotus' narrative strongly suggests that Alcmaeon's visit to Sardis preceded and led directly to his victory at the Olympic games. There is evidence that this Olympic victory took place in 592.[17] Alcmaeon's visit to Sardis was probably in the 590s during the reign of Alyattes (c.610–560) and was connected to the former's attempt to win Lydian aid for the Sacred War.[18]

How could Alcmaeon lead the Athenian forces in the Sacred War if he was both accursed and banished? George Forrest's interpretation is attractive: that the Sacred War was fought 'for the possession of' not 'for the sake of' Delphi.[19] According to this scenario Alcmaeon and his allies fought against the established order at Delphi, defeated it and set up a new organization that was sympathetic to the conquerors. The Alcmaeonids who were formerly the victims of Delphi were, by the middle of the sixth century, among its strongest supporters. This interpretation might also explain how the Alcmaeonids won their reacceptance into Athens.

Another problem with Herodotus' narrative is that Alcmaeon's son Megacles II was invited to court the daughter of Cleisthenes, the tyrant of Sicyon, on the basis of the wealth and fame that the family had already won with the aid of Croesus. The marriage of Megacles II and Agariste I can be dated with reasonable certainty between 575 and 571 and probably in 575, more than a decade before Croesus became king of Lydia.[20]

Megacles II was the head of the family in the 560s and 550s as leader of the Paralioi or Shore faction in Athens. Megacles II alternately supported and opposed the rise of the tyrant Pisistratus to power in Athens. The tyrant married a daughter of Megacles II, but then refused to have intercourse with her κατὰ νόμον. Herodotus says that Pistratus did not wish to have children by her because he already had grown sons, and because he feared the Alcmaeonid curse.[21] This incident caused a break between the two families. Pisistratus was eventually successful and was firmly in control of Athens by 546.

The next generation saw a temporary lull in the enmity between the two families. Megacles II's son Cleisthenes, the future legislator, became archon in 525/524 during the tyranny of Pisistratus' son Hippias.[22] He went into exile probably on the heels of the assassination of Hipparchus in 514. Cleisthenes used his influence at Delphi to secure the intervention of Sparta. He returned to Athens in 510 with the aid of Spartan troops under King Cleomenes. Cleisthenes 'took the people into his party', and his rival Isagoras called on Cleomenes to return and drive out the accursed.[23] Cleomenes returned, but with only temporary success. Cleisthenes pushed through his reforms but then dropped out of the picture after *c*.507. He may have died at this time. There is evidence that Cleisthenes tried to make an alliance with Persia, perhaps as protection against the Spartans.[24] A late tradition said that he was ostracized.[25] This idea has been generally rejected. Still, the rumour that the Alcmaeonids became 'Medizers' was a persistent one. It was brought up again at the time of the battle of Marathon.[26] Whether for this reason or some other, the Alcmaeonids did not muster the same degree of authority in the fifth century that they had enjoyed in the sixth. Pericles and Alcibiades, it will be remembered, were not Alcmaeonids.

In addition to Cleisthenes and the daughter who married Pisistratus (whose name we do not know), the children of Megacles II and Agariste I included Megacles III and Hippocrates. Hippocrates was the father of Agariste II, the mother of Pericles, and of Megacles IV, who was ostracized in 487/486. This Megacles was the father of Alcibiades' mother Deinomache and yet another Megacles (V). Deinomache probably married Alcibiades' father Cleinias about 451 or shortly before.[27] Their marriage was brief, for Cleinias died at the battle of Coronea in 447 or 446.[28]

## The family of Cleinias

The family of Alcibiades' father was not as distinguished as that of his mother, but it held a secure place in the Athenian aristocracy. Isocrates said that they belonged to the Eupatridae.[29] εὐπατρίδης means 'of noble family' (*LSJ*). Whatever else this term may or may not mean is a very complex and controversial problem. A discussion of the terms 'genos' and 'Eupatridae', and of any possible relationship that Alcibiades may have had with either, will be found in an appendix. The genealogy of this family is also a matter of some controversy. It must be decided how many generations intervened between Alcibiades, the friend of Cleisthenes, and Alcibiades, the subject of this biography (see Figure 2, the stemma, 'The Family of Cleinias'). Plutarch says that Cleinias fought at Artemisium (480) and died fighting the Boeotians at Coronea.[30] Dittenberger's objections to this statement have found wide acceptance.[31] It is unlikely that the same man fought at Artemisium and Coronea. One would expect that a man who equipped and led a trireme into battle would be at least thirty years old. That he would father his first child at the age of sixty is unlikely. That he would die in battle at the age of sixty-four, under the command of another man, thirty-four years after he had led his own command, also seems unlikely.

In 1952 Eugene Vanderpool published ostraka that were used against both Alcibiades the Elder (Alcibiades II) and Alcibiades the younger (Alcibiades III).[32] Both men had fathers named Cleinias. This seemed to fit in with most (but not all, as we shall see below) of the ancient evidence. Lysias, speaking against Alcibiades' son (Alcibiades IV), says that his great-grandfather (Alcibiades II) was ostracized.[33] Pseudo-Andocides says that

The Family of Cleinias

Alcibiades I
|
Cleinias I
(fought at Artemisium)
|
Alcibiades II
(ostracized 460)

Cleinias II = Deinomache     Axiochus
(died at Coronea in 446)          |
                              Cleinias III

Alcibiades III = Hipparete     Cleinias IV
|
Alcibiades IV
(Isoc. 16; Lysias 14, 15)

*Figure 2*

Alcibiades III's grandfather was ostracized.[34] When did this ostracism occur? Thucydides tells us that Alcibiades II renounced the Spartan proxeny.[35] Vanderpool created a convincing scenario to explain these facts by looking to the events of the late 460s.[36] After a major earthquake Sparta's helots revolted against their masters. Athens sent a large contingent under the pro-Spartan Cimon to help put down the slave rebellion. The Spartans grew suspicious of the Athenians' motives and asked them to leave. This action created a wave of anti-Spartan feeling in Athens.[37] Cimon was ostracized, probably in 461.[38] Vanderpool believed that Alcibiades II saw the writing on the wall and renounced his association with the Spartans. This renunciation came too late, however, and he was ostracized none the less in 460. Vanderpool produced, to my mind, convincing evidence from the ostraka that points to a date in the second quarter of the fifth century.[39] There was still one piece of ancient evidence, however, that his scheme did not satisfy. Isocrates described Alcibiades I, the friend of Cleisthenes, as the great-grandfather of the famous Alcibiades III.[40] Raubitschek and Bicknell (see Figure 3) sought to defend

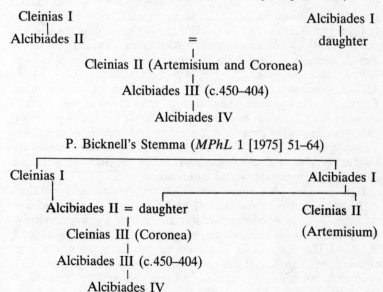

The Family of Cleinias According to Other Scholars
A.E. Raubitschek's Stemma (*RhM* 98 [1955] 258–262)

Cleinias I                                                          Alcibiades I
    |                                                                     |
Alcibiades II                    =                          daughter

Cleinias II (Artemisium and Coronea)
    |
Alcibiades III (c.450–404)
    |
Alcibiades IV

P. Bicknell's Stemma (*MPhL* 1 [1975] 51–64)

Cleinias I                                                          Alcibiades I
    |                                                                     |
Alcibiades II = daughter                          Cleinias II
    |                                                          (Artemisium)
Cleinias III (Coronea)
    |
Alcibiades III (c.450–404)
    |
Alcibiades IV

*Figure 3*

the accuracy of this statement.[41] In order to do this they devised a scheme whereby Alcibiades I and Cleinias I were brothers. Alcibiades II must then have married his first cousin in a plan that seems both cluttered and incestuous. The accuracy of Isocrates 16.26 is not worth defending. In the same passage the orator describes Cleisthenes as Alcibiades III's maternal great-grandfather. Cleisthenes' brother Hippocrates was Deinomache's grandfather.[42] It is possible to invent a wild scheme to show how a daughter of Cleisthenes could have married her first cousin Megacles IV and thus defend the accuracy of Isocrates. But this is clearly not the case. We must accept the inescapable conclusion that the orator's genealogical calculations were vague and inexact.

With these problems resolved, we can attempt to reconstruct the family of Alcibiades' father. Alcibiades I (born c.550) was a friend of Cleisthenes and with him worked to expel the Pisistratids in 510.[43] His son Cleinias I (born c.525) fought at Artemisium in 480.[44] Herodotus notes the fact that Artemisium, although not a victory for the Greeks, was a personal triumph for Cleinias: 'of the Greeks, the Athenians were the bravest; and of the Athenians Cleinias, son of Alcibiades, who supplied a ship with two hundred men, all at his own expense.'[45] His son Alcibiades II renounced the Spartan proxeny and was probably ostracized in 460, as was argued above. Both Demosthenes (20.115) and Plutarch (*Ar.*27.2) mention a decree passed by him in favour of Aristides' children, but Davies has rightly questioned the authenticity of this decree.[46] Alcibiades II had two known sons.[47] Cleinias II died at the battle of Coronea. Many historians believe that he proposed an important decree (*IG* I³ 34 = *ML* 46) concerning the collection of the tribute of the Athenian Empire.[48] His brother Axiochus was implicated in the profanation of the Mysteries and fled Athens in 415.[49] He is probably the Axiochus who proposed the second decree honouring the Neapolitans of Thrace (*IG* I³ 101 = *ML* 89). His son Cleinias III appears in Plato's *Euthydemus* and two of the Socratic works of Xenophon, *Memorabilia* and *Symposium*.

It is possible that there was a close personal and political relationship between Cleinias II and Pericles.[50] If this Cleinias was the Cleinias who proposed the decree for the improvement of the collection of the tribute, he may have been a supporter of Pericles. There is also the matter of the guardianship of the children of Cleinias II. It was an unusual arrangement, for ordinarily the children would have been entrusted to the care of the father's family. Cleinias had a living brother, Axiochus, who may have been an unsuitable candidate for guardian, but the arrangement that was implemented would probably have required the active co-operation of both Cleinias II and Pericles.[51] Nepos had another explanation.[52] He suggested that Pericles married Deinomache. We do not know the name of Pericles' wife, but this suggestion, tempting as it is, will probably have to be rejected. Davies' arguments against it, that it is insupportable chronologically and that it probably would have surfaced in some other source (e.g. Plat. *I Alc.* 104b), are sound.[53]

## The era of Alcibiades' youth

Alcibiades was born during the last stages of the First Peloponnesian War, in which Athens first built up and then lost a considerable empire on the Greek mainland. His father died in an important battle of that war, the battle of Coronea, as a result of which the Athenians lost control of Boeotia. Shortly afterwards, they lost Megara. In 446/445 Athens signed a thirty-year peace treaty with the Peloponnesians. This treaty may have signalled the end of an Athenian land empire, but it left Athens in control over much of the Aegean. Alcibiades grew up during an exciting time. From the age of three until about the age of eighteen, he would have witnessed the building of the Parthenon. He was about twelve when the chryselephantine Athena by Phidias was placed inside her temple. He probably saw Sophocles' *Antigone* when it was first performed about 441. Euripides won his first victory at the Dionysia at about the same time and composed his *Alcestis* shortly after that. Unfortunately, our sources are not very illuminating for this period. The decade (445–435) in which Alcibiades grew from childhood to adolescence and beyond is one of the least adequately documented periods of the fifth century.

## Politics in the Age of Pericles

Alcibiades grew up in the household of Pericles during the time of that leader's greatest popularity and influence. But just when did the Age of Pericles begin? The question is important if we are to formulate an idea of what Pericles' policies were and whether Alcibiades was influenced by them. Plutarch says that Pericles was the most important leader in Athens for forty years, tracing his dominance back to 469. This is surely wrong, and no one today would place Pericles' ascendancy before 461, when Cimon was ostracized and Ephialtes was assassinated. Many historians, however, do see the beginning of Pericles' position as the dominant force in Athenian politics at this time. The implications of this idea are enormous. If Pericles was the most important leader in Athens by 461 or 460, we must assume that he was responsible for the policies that led to both the Egyptian campaign and the First Peloponnesian War. Beloch and Miltner have suggested that Cimon instigated the Egyptian expedition.[54] Indeed, it does seem the sort of campaign that would appeal to Cimon. But, as Gomme has pointed out, it is absurd to assume that Pericles, who worked for Cimon's ostracism,[55] would feel obliged to carry out his policy in Egypt for six years while reversing it in every other arena.[56] The truth is that we know too little about the internal politics of Athens at this time to make many sweeping generalizations. It may be that Pericles was only one of several politicians who competed for dominance at this time. His ascendancy may not have begun before 454[57] or even 446.[58]

Several dubious tendencies seem to be at work here. One is an overly neat systematization of ideology. Cimon is always and only anti-Persian. Pericles is portrayed as the indefatigable anti-Spartan warrior. Politics is seldom that simple and clear-cut, and there is some evidence that Pericles and Cimon occasionally worked in concert.[59] Pericles was an opportunist, like all successful politicians, and it is not unthinkable that he might seek to increase the wealth of the Athenian Empire at the expense of Persia if the right opportunity presented itself. There is also a tendency to read Thucydides' conservative portrait[60] back into his earlier career. But even in the later stages of his career, Pericles was capable of adventurism (the Corcyra incident) and harsh imperialistic measures (the Megarian Decree[61]). There is also a tendency among writers, both ancient and modern, to ascribe to Pericles an immaculate record of success. If the Egyptian campaign was a failure, it must have been Cimon's idea, not Pericles'. If the battle of Coronea was a decisive defeat, the idea must be ascribed to Tolmides rather than to Pericles.[62] The point is not to defame Pericles, but to try to see him as a real human being dealing with real issues in the often ugly arena of politics. No politician has ever had a perfect record, and Pericles was no exception.

It is always tempting and almost always misleading to compare the politics of ancient Athens with the politics of modern democracies. It is tempting because there is virtually no other society in the entire stretch of human history, of which we have any detailed knowledge, that operated on a democratic basis. It is misleading because the conditions of human existence were fundamentally different. Athenian democracy was limited to free male citizens, but this limitation was not greatly different from the democracy of the United States in the early nineteenth century, to the degree that both states ignored women and tolerated slavery. Athenian democracy was different in that it was a direct democracy, not a representative one. Anyone who was a citizen and who desired to do so could vote in the assembly, the legislative body of the state. The Industrial Revolution, in addition, created circumstances that permanently changed society. Our society is based on capitalism, factories, factory owners, and factory workers. Athenian society had all these elements, but they played a relatively insignificant role. Land and agriculture were the dominant characteristics of the ancient economy.[63] To be sure, there were great disparities in wealth, but social classes, in the modern sense, did not exist.[64]

Neither were there political parties in ancient Athens. The lines of demarcation between any one group and another were vague and fluid. Any individual issue was likely to bring forth a different configuration of supporters. And yet there must have been a difference of opinion between those who were primarily interested in seeing that the richest families kept their wealth and those who were willing, for whatever reason, to allow the poorer citizens a greater share of the wealth and a greater voice in the government. These divisions exist in all societies, and there is evidence that there was such a difference of opinion in the actions of the leaders of Athens in the fifth century.

Cleisthenes, as we have seen, 'took the people into his party'.[65] His purpose may have been simply to defeat his rival Isagoras, but in so doing, he created a precedent. The leaders of Athens during the first two-thirds of the fifth century all came from the aristocracy, but they differed in their attitudes about the extent to which the poorer citizens should participate in the running of the state. The Marxist historian might try to prove that every conflict in Athenian history masks some aspect of class warfare. This clearly is not true. There are other historians who would like to prove that every difference in Athenian public life was based on regional, or purely personal, motives.[66] This approach seems to me equally misguided.

It is generally assumed that Pericles, like Cleisthenes, his mother's uncle, took the side of the people in debates that did centre on the question of popular representation. The evidence for this may be doubted, but all the sources we have point in that direction, and none suggests that Pericles ever represented aristocratic privilege. The Funeral Oration[67] is not the exact reproduction of an actual speech, but it represents Thucydides' idea of the sort of thing Pericles would say on such an occasion. In this oration Pericles speaks with pride of the Athenian constitution, which is called a democracy, and he seems to approve of the fact that the government is in the hands, not of a minority, but of the whole people. He also approves of the laws of Athens, especially those that protect the oppressed. If we then call Pericles a democrat, we mean only that he accepted the Athenian constitution of his day and did not seek to alter it. Indeed, if we can accept the spirit of the speech that Thucydides has put into the mouth of Pericles, it would seem that Pericles not only accepted democracy, but that he championed it.

Aristotle's *Constitution of the Athenians* also gives us a portrait of Pericles as a spokesman for the popular class. Aristotle, to be sure, did not approve of democratic reform, but that alone is no reason to discount his testimony. Pericles is said to have fought against the aristocratic privileges of the Areopagus and to have urged a naval policy that would provide jobs and power for the poor.[68] Aristotle also says that Pericles instituted pay for jury service, making it possible for the poor to take part in the judicial system.[69]

Some of Aristotle's details may be open to question, but the general portrait that he draws is consistent with the information that we get from other sources. Plutarch draws on Aristotle in his life of Pericles, but he also maintains that 'many other writers' have said that Pericles passed programmes for the benefit of the common people, including payment for public services and the waiving of the price of admission for the city's festivals.[70] Plutarch, to be sure, reflects the usual aristocratic bias of ancient historians when he says that these measures led the people to become 'extravagant and undisciplined',[71] but this prejudice should not blind us to the fact that Plutarch read many writers who believed that Pericles was an advocate of democratic reform. Plutarch also quotes Thucydides' statement that, in the hands of Pericles, Athens was nominally a democracy, but was actually under the control of the first citizen.[72] This is not evidence that Pericles had oligarchic sympathies. Thucydides admired Pericles' firmness and ability to control, and even contradict, the people, but Pericles' true strength lay in his ability to persuade, not in any constitutional powers that he held. Pericles was a general, one of ten, and subject to re-election every year. If Pericles was a 'first citizen', it was only by common consent. The people could remove him from power at any time, and on one occasion they did just this.[73]

Pericles could not have maintained the power that he held for twenty or thirty years through 'personal and family friendships', as Sealey suggests.[74] If the majority of Athenians looked to him as their leader and revered his memory as they did no other politician of that era, he must have offered them more than a list of his friends and ancestors. He must have endorsed some coherent political stance, no matter how flexibly.

Pericles' political platform, if we can trust any of our ancient sources, stressed democratic reform, a strong navy, and jobs and pay for the poor. Pericles supported a public works programme that included the Parthenon and other buildings whose remains still stand on the acropolis of Athens.[75] This programme, which was very controversial at the time, also created jobs for the poor. Pericles was an unapologetic advocate of empire, and he took an unfriendly stance with respect to Sparta.[76] Pericles, as we stated previously, was a politician and doubtless a flexible one. He was capable of changing his mind and of exploiting opportunities as they arose. It is unlikely that he believed in any inflexible ideological system, but it does seem likely that he supported a loose political platform based on some of the principles just outlined.

The Athenian democracy was fuelled by the Athenian Empire. The benefits of the empire were considerable for the poor; the empire created the jobs in the navy and on the building programmes and helped to finance the pay that was given to jurors and public officials. M.I. Finley has given us a vivid picture of how the empire benefited the poor, and how 'the full democratic system of the second half of the fifth century BC would not have been introduced' without it.[77] Rewards for the rich were not so obvious. 'There were no Athenian entrepreneurs to exploit tea or cotton plantations, to mine gold or diamonds, to build railroads or jute mills in the subject territories.'[78] There was more than a casual link among those leaders, like Pericles, who promoted democratic reform at home and a forceful policy of imperialism abroad.

It would be only natural for Alcibiades to follow in the footsteps of his famous guardian. Alcibiades, like all politicians, had to seek out his constituency, and that process may have involved a few false steps. If Alcibiades ever sought to regain the Spartan proxeny or to arrange a peace treaty between Athens and Sparta,[79] these were surely false starts and were motivated by an opportunistic desire to gain political prominence. Thucydides

13

dropped these suggestions into the speech that he wrote for Alcibiades to deliver at the time that he defected to the Spartans in the year 415/414.[80] It is possible that Thucydides, also an exile, might have heard this speech or, if not, that he could have received a reasonably accurate report of it, since he seems to have been in the Peloponnese for much of his exile.[81] The speech is not verbatim, but it is definitely in character, and it seems to be consistent with what Alcibiades would have said. Since Alcibiades was trying to gain the Spartans' confidence and to insinuate himself into their service, there was every reason for him to minimize his democratic leanings and to suggest as much common ground with them as he could. Yet Thucydides put the following words into his speech.

> Or if anyone thought the worse of me because I was rather on
> the side of the people, here again he should see that this was
> no good reason for being against me. My family has always
> been opposed to dictators; democracy is the name given to any
> force that opposes absolute power; and so we have continued
> to act as the leaders of the common people.[82]

It would be only natural, as we have stated, for Alcibiades to follow the political platform that had proved so successful for Pericles, his cousin and guardian. It is our contention that Alcibiades was favourable to Athens' democratic system in that he adhered to and often prospered under the Athenian constitution. It is true that Thucydides has Alcibiades call democracy 'acknowledged folly'[83] in the same speech that has just been discussed. Alcibiades, if he said this to the Spartans, was fighting for his political future, if not his life, and was perhaps justifiably bitter over the fact that the Athenians had recalled him, caused him to be exiled, and sentenced him to death. It is indeed conceivable that Alcibiades, who was a known companion of Socrates and his circle, might have held some secret disdain for democracy. However, there is no real evidence for this,[84] and it really does not matter. The public platform of Alcibiades is our concern, not his private thoughts or motivation. Alcibiades is often called an opportunist. He was unquestionably ambitious, and, yes, he was an opportunist, but he held no monopoly on this characteristic. Themistocles, Pericles, Alexander, and Caesar were also opportunists. Alcibiades differed from these great men primarily in that he was less successful than they. He may have been as brilliant, but he was finally unable to implement his schemes.

The portrait of Alcibiades that has come down to us, in spite of his association with Socrates, is not that of an intellectual. He was a man of action, and action meant warfare and politics. Alcibiades wanted the mantle of Pericles, he wanted power in Athens, and the only logical path toward that goal was the adoption of Pericles' political platform. Like Pericles, Alcibiades, perhaps after the few false steps mentioned above, adopted an attitude of hostility toward Sparta. The Quadruple Alliance of 420 and the policy that led up to the battle of Mantinea are evidence of that. If, as seems likely, Alcibiades was a member of the commission to reassess the tribute in 425/424 (see pp. 30–1). then he supported a forceful stance with respect to the Athenian Empire.[85] His advocacy of the Sicilian expedition represents a policy that should have enlarged the empire, strengthened the navy, and created new jobs for the poor. Nicias represented a different political attitude. He opposed the Sicilian expedition, and he had been the chief proponent of peace with Sparta. Thucydides says that Nicias wanted to preserve his fine record as general and statesman and believed that he could best do that by avoiding war.[86]

In the speech that Thucydides gives him to deliver to the Spartans, Alcibiades says that he, like his family before him, has always worked to be a leader of the people, but that he wanted to lead them in a moderate, not in a licentious way, like the leaders who drove him out of Athens.[87] This is an important point that needs some consideration.

## Alcibiades and the demagogues

Pericles, during the latter stages of his career, was able to work from a broad consensus. He was able to draw support from a wide variety of constituents, from a political conservative like the historian Thucydides, who saw him as a benevolent despot, to the more extreme supporters of the poor. Isocrates called him a demagogue.[88] This was not an insult. The Greek word *demagogos* meant simply 'leader of the people', and was not invariably used in a negative way in the ancient world.[89] According to Finley, it is not a word commonly used by our sources.[90] To be sure, aristocratic writers such as Thucydides, Xenophon and Aristotle did characterize the popular leader or radical democrat as invariably avaricious, violent, vicious, and wretched. Their prejudice lives on in our use of the word 'demagogue', a pejorative and loaded term like 'carpetbagger' or 'scalawag'. Modern American historians of the Reconstruction have ceased to use these terms. The term 'scalawag', for instance, implied that all white Southern Republicans during Reconstruction were opportunistic traitors. The term 'demagogue' is equally prejudicial. It implies that all popular leaders were violent and unscrupulous. Some undoubtedly were, but surely not all.[91] However, it is difficult to find a substitute for this term: 'radical leader' implies too much, 'popular leader' too little. Pericles and Alcibiades were 'popular leaders', but they were not 'demagogues'. Whatever we choose to call it, a new phenomenon began in Athens with the career of Cleon. The demagogues of the last third of the fifth century were leaders of the people who were not born of the aristocratic class. Pericles obviously does not qualify, nor does Alcibiades. But Pericles was a transitional figure and pioneered many of the techniques perfected by Cleon.[92]

Cleon is clearly the key figure in this movement, and, as Thucydides says, 'he exercised a great influence over the people'.[93] He represented an even more forceful policy of imperialism than Pericles had, and there was a definite difference in style. Pericles' cool, aristocratic reserve won him the epithet 'Olympian'.[94] Cleon's style must have been more emotional and more direct. He influenced Alcibiades as well as his own immediate followers.[95] Indeed Cleon's influence reaches down to the orator Demosthenes and beyond.[96]

According to Aristotle,[97] there was an unbroken line of radical leadership after Cleon throughout the rest of the fifth century. This line surely included Hyperbolus, Androcles, and Cleophon. Although the comic poets and other writers represented them as poor, obscure, and even foreign-born, they were according to the research of Connor, probably *nouveaux riches*.[98] They were often the sons of wealthy manufacturers, but they probably spent most of their time pursuing political careers.[99] The point here is that Alcibiades could never hope to recapture the old coalition of Pericles. He had to find some ground between the radical demagogues, such as Hyperbolus and Androcles, and the conservative democrats, such as Nicias. Alcibiades seems to have underestimated the importance of the demagogues, and it is likely that one of them, Androcles, was instrumental in engineering his downfall in 415 (see pp. 58–62).[100]

This discussion of Athenian politics in the late fifth century owes much to Hignett, with whom I am in basic agreement.[101] Where we disagree, it is primarily a matter of semantics. Hignett distinguishes only oligarchs, moderates, and radicals. Athens in the fifth century was a democracy. To be an active participant in the arena of politics, one had to work within the framework of the democracy. True oligarchs, such as Critias and Antiphon, were relatively few in number. Intellectually they may have had a great influence, especially on politicians who were less interested in democratic reforms, but they were outside the mainstream of Athenian politics. They represented only a small minority of subversive and disgruntled extremists. They were able to come to power in 411 and 404 only under extraordinary circumstances. The average wealthy and patriotic landowner would probably support a politician like Nicias who seemed less enthusiastic in expanding the empire or pursuing other programmes that would benefit the poor.

## Anecdotes about Alcibiades' youth

There are a number of isolated facts and anecdotes about Alcibiades' youth. Plutarch tells us, on the authority of Antisthenes, that his nurse was a Spartan woman named Amycla.[102] We do not know whether a Spartan nurse was unusual, but there were several factors that linked Alcibiades with Sparta. His family had held the position of proxenos of Sparta. The proxenos, a highly prized position that was often held by a single family and passed down from generation to generation,[103] was a person who looked after the interests of a foreign people. Alcibiades II had renounced the proxeny, apparently during a period of strong anti-Spartan feeling.[104] His grandson, early in his political career, tried unsuccessfully to get it back. His family had strong ties with the family of the Spartan ephor Endius, whose father's name was Alcibiades.[105] Alcibiades was, in origin, a Laconian name.[106]

According to some accounts, Alcibiades and his younger brother Cleinias IV were put under the joint guardianship of Pericles and his brother Ariphron. Two anecdotes survive concerning Ariphron and his role as guardian to the two boys. Cleinias, according to Plato, was sent to Ariphron to remove him from Alcibiades' corrupting influence, but after six months Ariphron sent him back to Pericles, not knowing what to do with him.[107] This episode tells us more about Cleinias than about Ariphron. Cleinias was apparently a very troublesome delinquent.[108] Plato has Alcibiades, his own brother, call him a madman.[109] The other story comes to us from Plutarch[110] by way of an abusive oration that was attributed to Antiphon[111] but is lost to us. The oration was probably not actually written by Antiphon.[112] The story tells how Alcibiades ran away from home to spend some time with his lover Democrates. Ariphron wanted to make a public spectacle of the incident, but Pericles talked him out of it. Plutarch himself doubted the accuracy of this story, and it has generally been rejected. It is possible, however, that Alcibiades did have a lover named Democrates.[113] On the basis of these two stories, it is reasonable to conclude, as did Hatzfeld,[114] that Ariphron probably did have some role in the guardianship of these two boys, but that his role was of considerably less importance than that of Pericles.

The childhood anecdotes about Alcibiades seem designed to show that he was spoiled or charming or that he was trying very hard to get attention. One story tells how he and a group of his friends were playing a game in the road.[115] The Greeks played a game with the knucklebones of cloven-hoofed animals that was similar to dice. A wagon came down the road and threatened to run over Alcibiades' knucklebones. He stood up and ordered the driver to stop. When he did not do so, the other boys jumped out of the way. Alcibiades lay down in the road, daring the driver to run him over. The driver managed to stop at the last minute, but not without alarming a number of spectators. Another story tells how Alcibiades cut off his dog's tail.[116] His friends asked him why he did it since all Athens was condemning him for it. Alcibiades replied that he wanted people to talk about it or else they would be accusing him of something worse. Plutarch tells the story of how Alcibiades bit his opponent's arm during a wrestling match that he was losing.[117] When his adversary quipped that he bit like a woman, Alcibiades replied: 'No, like a lion.' These stories may all be apocryphal, but they are the sorts of thing that the Athenians were willing to believe about Alcibiades. They probably tell us something about his character. His actions were outrageous, yes, but they were performed with panache.

Pericles chose one of his oldest servants to be Alcibiades' tutor, a man named Zopyrus the Thracian.[118] Music was an important part of every upper-class Greek's education. Pericles' music teacher Damon remained one of his closest advisers.[119] The lyre and the aulos[120] were the most prominent instruments in Athenian education. A popular anecdote says that Alcibiades admired the lyre but refused to learn the aulos for fear that it would spoil his looks.[121] Alcibiades' refusal led to a decline in the use of the aulos in Athenian education.[122]

There are many stories of Alcibiades' amorous exploits. One of them involves Anytus,[123] a man later notorious as one of the prosecutors of Socrates in 399. Anytus, who was infatuated with Alcibiades, invited him to dinner. Alcibiades refused, but later, when he got drunk with some of his companions, decided to go anyway. Without so much as greeting his host, Alcibiades ordered his slaves to carry off half of Anytus' gold and silver. Instead of being angry at Alcibiades, Anytus defended him to his friends. He would have allowed Alcibiades to have everything. Like most of these anecdotes, this one is difficult to either prove or disprove. Although Littman does not deny the possibility that this anecdote might actually have occurred, he gives an excellent reason for doubting its accuracy: 'As the prosecutor of Socrates, Anytus was the possible subject of much vilification . . . it is very possible that some Socratic source or some writer made him the fawning lover of Alcibiades.'[124]

Another lover, we are told, sold everything he had and offered to give it to Alcibiades.[125] Alcibiades helped this man to earn a considerable profit by outbidding the tax-farmers, who would bid for the collection of public revenues with the money they had earned the preceding year. If they were to lose one year's bid, they would probably be out of a job. The tax-farmers bribed the man, as Alcibiades knew they would, and the man earned a talent for his efforts. Littman has tentatively identified this man, a metic, as Pulytion, who was later associated with Alcibiades in the profanation of the Mysteries.[126] Plutarch tells this story immediately after the one about Anytus. The juxtaposition was probably deliberate.[127] The first episode shows Alcibiades as a wild youth, carousing at night. The second episode shows Alcibiades being kind to a man of no great social standing and for no ulterior motive. The juxtaposition of the two stories might imply that they happened at about the same time, but the second event was probably considerably later.[128]

The most scandalous anecdotes come from Athenaeus. He tells us, on the authority of Antisthenes, that Alcibiades had carnal relations with his mother, his sister and his daughter.[129] This has been generally rejected both because it seems an outrageous libel and because there is no other evidence to suggest that Alcibiades had a sister. Antisthenes was a follower of Socrates and perhaps the founder of the Cynic school of philosophy.[130] The Socratics tended to hold Alcibiades partly responsible for the condemnation of their master. Athenaeus also mentions the *Axiochus* of Aeschines the Socratic, which portrayed Alcibiades in a continual state of drunkenness and in habitual pursuit of other men's wives.[131] Further, Athenaeus relates two stories about Alcibiades' amorous adventures in the city of Abydus on the Hellespont. The first story is attributed to [Antiphon].[132] This authority asserted that, as a young man, Alcibiades sailed to Abydus to learn more about the ways of love from the licentious women who lived there. Later, according to [Lysias],[133] he and his disreputable uncle Axiochus sailed to Abydus because they had heard of a beautiful woman in that city named Medontis. They found her, made love to her, and left her pregnant. When Medontis' daughter was grown, Athenaeus continues, Alcibiades and Axiochus returned to Abydus, and both men made love to her, each claiming that the other man was her real father. These stories do not inspire much credibility, both because of their fantastic nature and because of their obvious partisan bias. They probably do indicate that Alcibiades had a reputation for prodigious erotic activity.[134] Such a reputation is common for a person of great physical beauty.[135] But there is no reason to doubt that Alcibiades had many lovers of both sexes.

### Alcibiades and Socrates

Socrates was, of course, the most famous of Alcibiades' lovers. They seem to have known each other from a time when Alcibiades was quite young. Plato's *Protagoras* takes place about 435 when Alcibiades would have been about fifteen, Socrates about thirty-five, and they seem to have already known each other for some time. In the opening scene of that dialogue an unnamed friend accuses Socrates of chasing Alcibiades and his youthful beauty, an accusation that Socrates does not deny. The friend says that Alcibiades is still good-looking although his first beard is beginning to grow. The friend goes on to ask how Alcibiades is treating Socrates. All this sounds like the typical Greek homosexual relationship.[136] The *I Alcibiades* takes place about three years later (*c*.432). Socrates describes himself as the first of all of Alcibiades' lovers. Socrates still loves him because he loves Alcibiades' soul; the others only loved his body.[137] Socrates neither confirms nor denies that he loves Alcibiades' body, but if the episode were told of any other individual in Athenian society that would be clearly implied. Scholars have generally rejected the notion that Socrates and Alcibiades were physical lovers for three reasons. First, Socrates, beginning with the writings of Plato, has taken on the aura of a religious figure. Whereas, for the Greeks, sainthood might not preclude an erotic nature, it does in the Christian tradition. Second, scholars in that tradition, especially since the Victorian era, have been wary of the whole concept of Greek homosexuality and especially as it applies to a 'saint' like Socrates. Typical of this trend is A.E. Taylor who saw Socrates' eros as a metaphor for the mystical temperament.[138] Third, Plato specifically denies it in the *Symposium*. The *Symposium* takes place some nineteen years after the *Protagoras* in the year 416.[139] In this dialogue Alcibiades casts himself in the role of the rejected lover and tells at length how he attempted unsuccessfully to seduce Socrates.[140] It is night at the house of Agathon, a tragic poet, who has just won the prize for his play at a dramatic festival. Over wine, each of his guests gives a speech in praise of love. Late in the party Alcibiades enters in an advanced state of inebriation. He notices that Socrates is sitting by Agathon and asks him why he has chosen to sit by the best looking man in the room. Socrates protests that since he fell in love with Alcibiades he has not been able to look at another man without arousing Alcibiades' jealousy. Socrates pretends to be afraid of Alcibiades' amorous frenzy and claims that Alcibiades can hardly keep his hands off him. This does not sound like a spiritual relationship. The scene in which Alcibiades attempts to seduce Socrates is straight out of comedy. The humour is based on a reversal of expectations. Socrates, as the older man, should be chasing the young and beautiful Alcibiades. The point is translated into heterosexual terms by K.J. Dover who imagines 'Socrates as a healthy man who converses tranquilly, and then falls soundly asleep, when a beautiful girl has crept naked under his blanket and put her arms around him'.[141]

The evidence from Plato is inconclusive. He tells us that Socrates and Alcibiades were lovers for a period in excess of twenty years. He reminds us on several occasions that Socrates felt a definite erotic attraction for handsome young men. The most explicit statement of this is in the *Charmides* 155c–e. Socrates describes how he happened to look down Charmides' cloak and, seeing the beauty of his body, was aroused. The only specific denial in Plato of a physical relationship between Socrates and Alcibiades comes in a passage that is so playful it borders on burlesque. Plato would have every reason to deny a close physical relationship between Alcibiades and his master. Many Athenians believed that Alcibiades' behaviour was a reflection of Socrates' teaching. Plato is careful to point out that Alcibiades' behaviour, or rather misbehaviour, was a result, not of Socrates' teaching, but rather of a deliberate attempt to flee from it.[142] Xenophon thought that Socrates' relationship with Alcibiades and Critias was the real cause of his trial and condemnation.[143] The accusation was implicit in the charge 'corrupting the youth' and could not be made explicit by the terms of the amnesty of 403. It is true that Plato's Socrates believes that spiritual love is on a higher plane than carnal love, but nowhere is physical love scorned as an unworthy pursuit. It is time to look at this phenomenon as it really was and not continue to read our own cultural prejudices into it. R.J. Littman has led the way in this respect in an excellent article, 'The loves of Alcibiades'.[144] He asserts that some ancient authorities thought that Socrates and Alcibiades were physical lovers.[145] He comes very close to this conclusion himself, but hedges somewhat, pleading a lack of evidence. There is no absolutely convincing evidence. But given his followers' reluctance to discuss Socrates' sexual nature, especially with a man they considered to be a traitor, it is certainly possible that this relationship was not recorded with absolute candour. Littman ended his investigation of the matter with a quote from Bion:[146] 'Bion . . . best summed up the matter when he remarked that if Socrates felt desire for Alcibiades and abstained, he was a fool; if he did not, his conduct was in no way remarkable.'[147]

Socrates must have had a profound influence on Alcibiades. Plato has Alcibiades in the *Symposium* speak of the experience of hearing Socrates: 'I have heard Pericles and other great orators, and I thought they spoke well, but I never had any similar feeling; my soul was not stirred by them.'[148] It is impossible to measure the nature of that influence. Socrates' disciples took many different paths, from the Cynic Antisthenes to the Idealist Plato. The nature of Socrates' teachings is a notoriously difficult problem, far too complex to discuss here. A few brief points will suffice. There are only two major contemporary accounts extant, those of Xenophon and Plato.[149] Most historians would now reject Xenophon's portrait of Socrates as a simple, homespun philosopher although many details of his account are worthy of consideration. That leaves Plato. How much of Plato's portrait is the real Socrates, and how much is Plato? Opinions differ dramatically. A.E. Taylor thought that Plato's own philosophy, as opposed to Socrates', was revealed only in the later dialogues, such as the *Timaeus* and the *Laws*.[150] Others think that elements of Plato's philosophy can be seen even in the very early works such as the *Crito*.[151] We will probably never know for certain. But it is clear that Socrates was not primarily interested in a coherent set of dogmas.

He was interested in a method for the thorough examination of ideas. He seldom offered definitive answers to anything. Hippias in one of Xenophon's dialogues refuses to answer Socrates: 'unless you first declare your own opinion about the nature of Justice; for it's enough that you mock at others, questioning and examining everybody, and never willing to render an account yourself or to state an opinion about anything'.[152]

It should not be surprising, then, that many of Socrates' contemporaries confused him with the Sophists. He resembled them in many ways. He differed from them apparently in that he thought that there was a definitive answer to the questions that he continually posed, and they did not. But this similarity to the Sophists does not fully explain Aristophanes' caricature of Socrates in the *Clouds*. There, Socrates seems more interested in the pursuit of scientific knowledge than in ethical concerns. It has been suggested that Socrates was initially interested in scientific philosophy and only later, after 'a spiritual crisis', when he was near the age of forty (*c.*430), became interested in ethical problems.[153] This theory goes a long way to explain otherwise conflicting facts in Socrates' life and seems to be confirmed in Plato's *Phaedo* 96a–100a. If this theory is true, then it is interesting to note that Alcibiades knew Socrates several years before his 'conversion', and he may have known Socrates better as a scientist than as a spiritual teacher.

It would be foolish to suggest that Alcibiades was a credit to Socrates. Alcibiades was a public man for whom philosophy was of only minor importance. If the portrait of Socrates in the *Crito* is accurate, the philosopher would not have approved of Alcibiades' decision to defect to Sparta in 415. But both men lived in an age of great uncertainty. Both men challenged the stale dogma of their day and sought new alternatives. Both men were loved by their contemporaries and yet were feared as profound threats to the status quo. Dover notes in discussing Alcibiades' speech in Thucydides 6.16–18 that Alcibiades was 'capable of elaborate sophistry . . . and even perhaps of adapting contemporary scientific doctrines'.[154] Assuming again that this speech resembles one that Alcibiades actually made, it is not improbable that Alcibiades learned both science and sophistry from Socrates.

Chapter two

# Alcibiades and the early stages of the Peloponnesian War

Alcibiades' adult life coincided almost exactly with the Peloponnesian War. He did not become an important leader in Athens until after the Peace of Nicias, but he participated in the war from the beginning.[1] When Athens sent aid to Corcyra in 433, Alcibiades was about seventeen years old, and when the Peace of Nicias was signed in 421, he was probably twenty-nine. We know that he fought in the Potidaean campaign in 432 and in the battle of Delium in 424, but it is probable that he took part in other operations in the early stages of the war. Alcibiades began his active political career (an event that will be discussed later in this chapter) around 425 when he was about twenty-five, but there can be little doubt that he had aspirations, from an early age, to rise to a position of leadership.[2] Before the advent of the demagogues, politics and the military were inextricably combined. All the major leaders in Athens, from Themistocles to Pericles, had also been generals. If this was the case in times of relative peace, it was even more so during wartime. Although we cannot pinpoint Alcibiades' whereabouts during most of the Archidamian War, it is important to understand that these events greatly influenced his life and emerging political career. He undoubtedly took a keen interest in these events even where he did not take an active part.

## The Potidaean campaign

Even before the war actually began, Alcibiades took part in the campaign against Potidaea. Potidaea was a colony of Corinth, but a tributary ally of Athens. Athens and Corinth were on bad terms as a result of the Corcyrean episode, in which Athens sided with a Corinthian colony against the mother city. Shortly after the battle of Sybota in 433, in which a Corinthian fleet was defeated by a combined force of Athenians and Corcyreans,[3] Athens

24

demanded that Potidaea relinquish its system of accepting magistrates from Corinth, send hostages to Athens, and tear down its fortification to the south.[4] With the hope of Spartan[5] and Corinthian aid, and with the alliance of several neighbouring cities, the Potidaeans revolted from the Athenian Empire, perhaps in early June 432.[6] Before the Athenians had even heard of the revolt, they sent out a naval force against King Perdiccas of Macedonia. Archestratus, the commander of these ships, was also instructed to enforce the ultimatum against Potidaea by taking hostages and destroying its fortification. The Athenian force found itself unable to deal with both problems and so concentrated its efforts against Macedonia. Meanwhile a group of Corinthian volunteers and Peloponnesian mercenaries under the command of Aristeus set out to aid the rebels. Thucydides tells us that they reached their destination forty days after the revolt of Potidaea, perhaps in July 432.

When the Athenians learned of the revolt and the Peloponnesian aid, they sent reinforcements under Callias, the son of Calliades. The two contingents joined together, made peace with Perdiccas and marched on to Potidaea. The Athenians won the ensuing battle of Potidaea, probably in September 432. The Athenian general Callias was killed in the battle. The victors set up a blockade, cutting off Potidaea from her allies to the north. In order to apply a complete siege, the Athenians sent out Phormio with reinforcements, perhaps in October 432. Phormio built a wall on the south side of the city that cut Potidaea off from the rest of the peninsula. Athenian ships completed the blockade by sea. The long siege, which brought on large-scale starvation and even cannibalism, lasted until the winter of 430/429. The defeated Potidaeans were allowed to leave the city with their wives, their children, a single garment, and little else.

Alcibiades must have left on the expedition under either Archestratus or Callias, although Isocrates states that he went with Phormio.[7] In the *Symposium*, Plato allows Alcibiades himself to describe how he and Socrates went together as messmates on campaign to Potidaea. They were cut off at least once from their supplies and were forced to go without food. Socrates was better able to withstand hardships than anyone else on the campaign. Once, during a severe winter frost, Socrates, wearing no shoes and only his ordinary clothes, sustained a difficult march better than the other men who had shoes and warmer clothes. One summer day Socrates stood contemplating a problem and did not move from his spot until he had solved it at the dawn of the next day. Socrates saved Alcibiades' life in the battle. Alcibiades was wounded, and Socrates stayed by him, saving both his life and his armour. The generals conferred a prize of honour on Alcibiades that he thought should have been given to Socrates.

There are a number of chronological problems with this story. Isocrates, it was noted above, said that Alcibiades went to Potidaea with Phormio. Phormio did nothing more than ravage the countryside, which cannot be reconciled with a battle that Plato calls 'very severe'.[8] It is likely that Isocrates in this instance, as in so many others, is incorrect. He may have wanted, as Hatzfeld suggested,[9] to associate Alcibiades with the name of one of Athens' most successful generals. Unfortunately, the problems do not end with Isocrates. Plato does not seem to be consistent with himself. In the *Charmides*, Socrates is described as having just arrived from the battle of Potidaea. The people in Athens have just heard of the battle, and they press Socrates for details of what seems to be a very recent event. But in the *Symposium*, Plato tells us that Socrates took part in a winter campaign. This winter campaign had to either precede or come after the battle, and the most probable inference is that it was the beginning of the long seige of Potidaea that took place after the battle in September.

Why is this the most probable inference? What are the arguments against the idea that the winter campaign preceded rather than followed the battle? Certainly, we cannot derive a firm chronology from Plato's *Symposium*. Is it possible that the expedition under Archestratus, which we would date to June 432, actually left much earlier, perhaps in September 433?[10] Is it possible that this expedition included Alcibiades and Socrates, that it spent the winter of 433/432 in Macedonia and that this is the winter campaign that Plato mentions in the *Symposium*? Thucydides' narrative alone is loose enough to allow such an interpretation,[11] but there is other evidence that along with Thucydides dictates against this idea. Thucydides says that when the Athenians under Archestratus arrived in Thrace, they found Potidaea already in revolt.[12] We know from the tribute lists that the Potidaeans paid their tribute in the spring of 432,[13] and so the revolt could not have begun before about June 432. And since the expedition left at about the same time, neither could it have departed before about June 432.

Nor is it likely that Plato had some other winter campaign in mind in the *Symposium*. He has Alcibiades say that he and Socrates were messmates on the Potidaean campaign, and then goes on to describe the hardships that Socrates bore. He went hungry without complaining. He drank little, but when he did, he outdrank everyone without showing any signs of drunkenness. 'But it was in his endurance of winter – in those parts the winters are awful – that I remember, among his many marvelous feats.'[14] It is clear then that these events all happened on the Potidaean campaign. The *Symposium* is one of Plato's most polished dialogues. It is inconceivable that he would begin to discuss the Potidaean campaign and a few sentences later, without changing the context, discuss winter in the region with reference to another locale.

Plato's account in the *Symposium* is the more circumstantial, and it is the one that Plutarch followed in his life of Alcibiades. If this account cannot be reconciled with the one in the *Charmides*, it is the one to be preferred.[15] There are two hypothetical ways in which the accounts could be reconciled, but both ways present major difficulties. As discussed above, Archestratus could have spent the winter of 433/432 in Macedonia and only then proceeded to Potidaea in the spring. Thucydides' narrative seems to contradict this hypothesis since it says that Archestratus arrived in Thrace, found Potidaea in revolt, and only then proceeded to Macedonia. The other possibility is that the battle was fought in September; an early winter arrived in October and Socrates remained for a few weeks at the siege before returning to Athens. This explanation is also inadequate. October is not winter, and even if Socrates remained at Potidaea for only two weeks, news of the campaign would have preceded him back to Athens. The most logical conclusion is that Plato's account in the *Charmides* is not historically accurate. Alcibiades left Athens in the summer of 432, took part in the battle of Potidaea around September and probably returned in the winter of 432/431 since he had been wounded, even though the siege was to continue for two more years.

### The Archidamian war

The Potidaean and Corcyrean affairs and the Megarian Decree were major incidents that led to the declaration of war.[16] The war actually began in spring 431 with the Theban attack on Plataea. The causes of the war are complex and controversial. Thucydides' diagnosis, 'what made war inevitable was the growth of Athenian power and the fear which this caused in Sparta',[17] has led to much debate and speculation. Suffice it to say that there existed in Greece at this time two major powers whose government and whose temperament were very different. At the time of the

Persian Wars, Sparta was the most powerful Greek state. Since that time Athens had built up an empire and had challenged Sparta's pre-eminent position. Sparta's army was still justly considered the best in Greece. Her allies included Corinth, Megara, Thebes, and most of Boeotia, parts of western Greece such as Ambracia and Anactorion, parts of central Greece such as Phocis and Locris, and all the Peloponnese except the Argolis and most of Achaea.

Athens' advantages were different but potent. Her allies included Acarnania, Corcyra, Zacynthus, Plataea, and the Messenians of Naupactus. Of greater significance to Athens were the allies of her empire: most of the islands of the Aegean and many of the coastal cities of Thrace and Asia Minor. Unlike the allies of Sparta, most of Athens' allies were subservient. The Athenians did not have to deal with the independent aspirations of a Thebes or a Corinth. Athens' financial resources were extensive, and her navy was the best in the Greek world. Pericles' strategy emphasized avoiding land battles with the Spartans. This meant abandoning Attic farms and moving the rural population into the walled city during the Spartan attacks.

Pericles' policy has been generally admired by historians[18] although it inadvertently facilitated the spreading of the plague when it broke out in Athens in 430.[19] Pericles also recommended, according to Thucydides, that the Athenians not attempt to add to their empire or engage in any dangerous enterprises while the war was in progress.[20] Many Athenians apparently found these restrictions difficult especially after the outbreak of the plague. Thucydides gives Pericles a speech in which he defends his policy against an apparently hostile audience.[21] The loss of farms, Pericles says, is not of great importance. What is important is that Athens has a great navy and can sail anywhere she wishes. Pericles tells the Athenians that they are fighting for their empire that they cannot afford to lose: 'your empire is now like a tyranny'.[22] Pericles may compare Athens to a tyrant but not to emphasize that her allies are 'tyrannized'. Rather the point is that once the position has been seized, it cannot be ignored or abandoned. Athens has no choice but to maintain its position or see the state in ruins. It is important to see that Pericles' policy was a war strategy and by no means a repudiation of imperialism.[23]

The first ten years of the Peloponnesian War are called the Archidamian War after King Archidamus of Sparta. The Archidamian War saw no traditional land battles between Athens and Sparta. The battles that were fought always involved some third power and usually took place in some remote region of the Greek world such as Potidaea, Amphipolis, or Corcyra.[24] The Greek states were not only divided between Athens and Sparta, but they were also divided among themselves, most states having a pro-Athenian and a pro-Spartan faction. The party out of power would be the one more likely to bring in a foreign state with the result that the invaded country would have to fight both a foreign nation and a dissatisfied portion of its own populace. The bitterness engendered by these frequently intense struggles led to atrocities and gave this conflict its peculiar characteristic. The Peloponnesian War was not just a conflict between nations but also a war of competing ideologies. Thucydides' narrative gives special emphasis to the civil war in Corcyra in 427. This bitter conflict resulted in massacres of both democrats and oligarchs and the intervention of both Peloponnesians and Athenians. Although the democratic faction eventually regained control, the primary result of this conflict was, in effect, to deprive Athens of a potentially valuable ally.

Athens also suffered the revolt of a much older ally, Mytilene, which had come to dominate most of the island of Lesbos. When the Athenians finally put down the revolt in 427, they voted to put to death the entire adult male population and to enslave the women and children. This severe penalty, which had its counterpart in the Peloponnesian retribution on the Plataeans occurring at about the same time, was reversed at the last minute after the Athenians had reconsidered the decision. Thucydides' 'Mytilenian Debate' between Cleon and Diodotus gives the reader a vivid interpretation of the issues at stake.[25]

The early years of the Archidamian War, although hardly decisive, had not gone well for the Athenians. An unusual set of circumstances in 425 conspired to improve the Athenian position. Demosthenes was the general who set these circumstances in motion. He fortified Pylos, a site on the west coast of Messenia, less than fifty miles from Sparta. In an attempt to dislodge Demosthenes, the Spartans placed a force of 420 hoplites with attendant helots on the island of Sphacteria, just south of Pylos. Demosthenes received reinforcements, and the Athenians besieged the Peloponnesians on the island. Under the leadership of Cleon they eventually brought back to Athens 292 hoplites of which 120 were full Spartan citizens. This was a major victory for Athens for a number of reasons. In the course of the Pylos campaign, Athens had taken over virtually the entire Spartan navy. They held the Spartan prisoners as insurance against any future invasions, threatening to kill them if the Spartans crossed the Attic border. But most of all, the Athenians had won a great psychological victory over the supposedly invincible Spartan army. The legend of the Spartans fighting to the last man, the legend of Thermopylae, had been dealt a serious blow. Needless to say, the reputations of Demosthenes and Cleon were enormously enhanced.

Demosthenes was one of the participants in, and may have been the architect of, an elaborate plan to conquer Boeotia. The plan involved the use of native Boeotians who wished to make their land a democracy. Demosthenes was to take the town of Siphae in the western part of Boeotia with the help of the local rebels. Hippocrates was to seize Delium in the east at about the same time, and from these two posts, the Athenians could divide and conquer the whole region. The scheme did not work. The Athenian plans were divulged to the Spartans, who informed the Boeotians, who were, in turn, ready for the attack. To make matters worse, someone, Thucydides does not say who, miscalculated the day of attack, and Demosthenes arrived early at a Siphae that had been occupied by a Boeotian army. Hippocrates did manage to fortify Delium, but he then had to face a formidable Boeotian army that had already secured its western front. Hippocrates had not heard of Demosthenes' failure in the west when he sent the majority of his troops back to Athens. The Thebans attacked and defeated the Athenians and the defeat was turned into a rout.

Alcibiades was present at this battle and in this rout. Thucydides says that some of the Athenians fled toward Delium and the sea, and that others fled toward Mount Parnes in the south or to any other direction away from the enemy. The Boeotians followed, killing many Athenians, and were stopped only by the night. Plato tells us that Alcibiades was in the cavalry, and that he observed the calmness and courage of Socrates, who was retreating on foot under the command of the general Laches.[26] In the dialogue that bears his name, Laches also commends Socrates for the courage he demonstrated during this disastrous retreat.[27]

## Alcibiades' career, marriage, and family

Alcibiades apparently had not achieved any great political eminence by 425. Aristophanes alludes to him in the *Acharnians*, produced in that year, as a young upstart, but not in such a way as to suggest that he was an important political leader at the time.[28] [Andocides] suggests that Alcibiades was a member of the commission of ten, set up to enlarge the assessment of the tribute from the allies.[29] This oration suggests that Alcibiades was the primary instigator of the commission. This is highly unlikely since he was only twenty-five at the time, but it is not unlikely that he was a member.[30] We have an inscription that gives us more details about this reassessment of the tribute.[31] The boule was to elect ten assessors (taktai) who would draw up a list of the allies to be assessed and a provisional amount for each. The allies would be allowed to state their case if they thought the assessment too high. This assessment seems to be considerably higher and to include a larger number of cities than before, but the actual amount of increase is difficult to judge since we have very little information concerning the assessment of 428. Most historians associate this augmentation of the tribute with Cleon,[32] both because of the generally threatening tone of the decree, and because it must have been passed soon after the victory at Sphacteria. Alcibiades was not the promoter of this plan, but if he participated in it, as seems highly possible, it would imply that he approved of the idea.

One of Plutarch's most colourful anecdotes[33] may be associated with this period of Alcibiades' life.[34] Plutarch called it his 'first entrance into public life'. Alcibiades was passing by the assembly one day and heard the sound of applause. He asked the reason for the applause and, when he was told that men were making contributions to the state, he agreed to make one himself. The audience greeted Alcibiades' contribution with enthusiasm, and he was so caught up in the moment that he forgot that he was hiding a quail in his cloak. The bird got away, and many of the delighted Athenians tried to recover it for Alcibiades. The quail was finally caught by the sea captain, Antiochus, who then became a lifelong favourite of Alcibiades. Indeed, as we shall see, Antiochus was present near the end of Alcibiades' days in the service of Athens, and may have inadvertently been responsible for his fall (see pp. 91–3). Both the commission for the enlargement of the tribute and voluntary contributions of money to the state belong to a period when Athens' treasury had been seriously depleted by six or more years of constant war.[35]

Two other anecdotes that may belong to this period concern Timon the misanthrope and Agatharchus the painter. Timon was probably a real person around whom much legend was attached. He is mentioned by Aristophanes[36] but is known to us primarily from much later writers.[37] Plutarch tells essentially the same story in the *Alcibiades* and in the *Antony* except that in the former, Timon and Alcibiades met only once, while in the latter, they were regular companions. In both accounts, however, Timon approves of Alcibiades' behaviour because he is certain that it will bring ruin to the city. In the other anecdote Alcibiades confined Agatharchus to his house and refused to let him leave until the artist had decorated it with his paintings. After the work was completed, Alcibiades rewarded him handsomely.[38] Agatharchus of Samos was an important painter of the middle to late fifth century, often thought to be the first to make extensive use of perspective.[39]

At some time in the late 420s Alcibiades married Hipparete, a member of one of Athens' wealthiest families.[40] (See Figure 4, 'The Family of Alcibiades' Wife'.) Her mother, whose name we do not know, had been Pericles' wife before she married Hipparete's father, Hipponicus.[41] Hipponicus was the son of the famous Callias II, who was Aristides' cousin and Cimon's brother-in-law. He fought at Marathon and performed various diplomatic functions for Athens. Some historians think that he concluded a peace treaty with Persia, but the authenticity of the 'Peace of Callias' must remain in doubt.[42] The family's fortune was based on its silver mines, its land-ownership, and its association with the Eleusinian Mysteries.[43] Hipponicus was known as the richest man in Greece.[44] He is mentioned by Thucydides as

The Family of Alcibiades' Wife

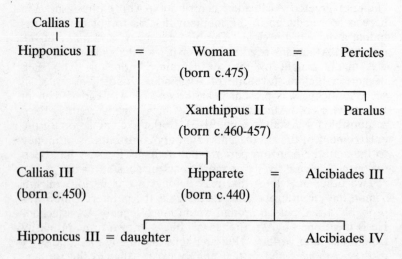

*Figure 4*

having taken part in a battle at Tanagra with Nicias in 426.[45] He seems to have married the divorced wife of Pericles around 455.[46] In addition to Hipparete, they had a son, Callias (the third of that name) who dissipated most of the family fortune through his attentions to sophists and women.[47] It was in the house of Callias III that Alcibiades and Socrates were reported to have met Protagoras.[48] According to Plutarch, Alcibiades struck Hipponicus once, not out of anger, but simply on a childhood dare.[49] When the incident threatened to become a public scandal, Alcibiades went to Hipponicus' home, removed his clothing and asked Hipponicus to punish him in whatever way he saw fit. Whether this incident contains a sexual implication is not clear, but the scheme was apparently successful. Hipponicus not only forgave Alcibiades; he gave him his daughter in marriage.

Plutarch gives us an alternative version of this story that is also found in [Andocides].[50] According to this version, it was not Hipponicus, but his son Callias III, who gave Hipparete in marriage to Alcibiades along with a dowry of ten talents.[51] Ten talents was an enormous amount at that time; and along with the additional ten talents that Alcibiades extorted from Callias III after the birth of a child, it may have been as [Andocides] called it, 'a dowry such as no Greek had ever obtained before'.[52] There can be little doubt that Alcibiades married Hipparete for her money.

Callias III became so worried that Alcibiades was after his money that he promised to bequeath it to the state if he died without heirs.[53] Alcibiades did not settle down to quiet domesticity, Plutarch's account continues, but rather he flaunted his affairs with both Athenian and foreign courtesans.[54] Hipparete went to live with her brother and later went to the archon to file for divorce.[55] Alcibiades went to the archon, met her, and physically removed her, carrying her through the agora to his home. Our sources disagree in their interpretation of this act. [Andocides] says that this act showed 'his contempt for the magistrates, the laws, and his fellow Athenians in general'.[56] Plutarch says that it was nothing of the sort, but rather it was the custom in divorce cases for the woman to go to the magistrate in order to give the husband a chance to seize her.[57]

The truth probably lies somewhere between the two versions. There was probably no custom of physically removing the wife who wanted a divorce,[58] but in this male-dominated society, the Athenian men would likely look on with tolerance or even with approval as Alcibiades, already noted for his outrageous behaviour, carried his rich wife back home. Plutarch says that

Hipparete lived with Alcibiades until her death, which occurred soon after, while Alcibiades was away on a trip to Ephesus.[59]

They had at least two children. A daughter, whose name we do not know, married her cousin Hipponicus III, son of Callias III, and was divorced by him, according to Lysias, because she was guilty of incest with her brother.[60] That brother was Alcibiades IV, who was probably born about 417 or 416.[61] There may have been an older son who died in infancy since, by the usual tradition, the eldest son would have been named Cleinias.[62]

Alcibiades IV faced a number of prosecutions when he came of age. Isocrates wrote a defence for him in a case that involved an alleged theft by Alcibiades (the father) of a team of racehorses. In the speech Alcibiades (the son) says that he was left an orphan by 'my father's exile and my mother's death'.[63] He was not quite four years old when his life was threatened in a matter that concerned his father's banishment. This matter must be the Spartan fortification of Decelea in 413, which gives us an approximate date for the birth of Alcibiades IV.[64] He was banished by the Thirty when he was about thirteen, and, when he returned to Athens in 403, he was not allowed to regain his property or given any compensation for it. The suit for which Isocrates wrote Alcibiades IV a defence (*c*.397) was followed about two years later (*c*.395) with a problem arising out of the conduct of Alcibiades IV during the Corinthian War. Lysias wrote two speeches for the prosecution, accusing the young man of avoiding military service and of deserting the ranks.[65] Nothing certain is known of Alcibiades IV after this date, although we know that he provided some ammunition for the comic poet Archippus: 'He walks with utter wantonness, trailing his long robe behind him, that he may be thought the very picture of his father, yes, he slants his neck awry, and overworks the lisp.'[66]

**To the peace of Nicias**

Alcibiades' only other known political activity at this time was his attempt to court the favour of the Spartan prisoners captured on the island of Sphacteria.[67] He sought to regain the position of proxenos held by his grandfather and to use this position as a means of establishing peace between the two powers. The Spartans, not surprisingly, chose to deal with Nicias, a far more stable, and, at the time, a far more influential statesman. Considering Alcibiades' apparent co-operation with the pro-war party, Hatzfeld calls this policy 'the deed of an opportunist who is feeling his way'.[68] This is a fair assessment if we consider the qualifications of 'opportunism' that were discussed in the first chapter. There is no evidence that Alcibiades worked closely with Cleon, although they may have agreed on certain policies. Alcibiades was certainly no ally of Nicias. Thucydides has Alcibiades tell the Spartans of his attempt to make peace in his speech to them after his defection from Athens in 415/414. He accuses the Spartans of dealing with his 'personal enemies, thus putting them in a stronger position and discrediting me'.[69] The 'personal enemies' can only mean Nicias and his cohorts. Alcibiades seems to have been looking for some political ground between Nicias and Cleon. To push for a vigorous prosecution of the war and at the same time to seek peace may not be consistent, but it is neither unusual in politics nor undesirable.

At any rate, Alcibiades was not allowed a major role in the creation of peace. This fact should not be surprising since he was probably still under thirty years of age. In 423 Nicias concluded a one-year truce with the Spartans that might have led directly to a peace treaty had it not been for the ambitions of the Spartan general Brasidas. Brasidas had already brought several important Athenian allies in and around the region of Thrace over to the Spartan camp by both diplomatic and military means. Chief of these cities was Amphipolis, which the Athenians considered essential to their security and well-being. Cleon was determined to recapture Amphipolis. The ensuing battle of Amphipolis was a Spartan victory, but it brought about the deaths of both Brasidas and Cleon. The two major proponents of war were dead, and so the negotiations for peace proceeded rapidly. The treaty signed in 421 was supposed to last for fifty years. Athens was to restore most of the land she had taken from Sparta including Pylos. Sparta and her allies were to return Argilus, Stagira, Amphipolis, Panactum, and other regions taken from the Athenians. Both sides were to return all prisoners of war. Alterations in the arrangements could be made by mutual consent of Athens and Sparta.

The war was temporarily over. Cleon was dead. Nicias had become Athens' most influential leader with no major rivals. The scene was set for Alcibiades' meteoric rise to the summit of Athenian political power.

Chapter three

# Alcibiades and the peace of Nicias, 421–416

## Problems with the peace of Nicias

Sparta, whose reputation had been tarnished in the Archidamian War, faced many problems both at home and abroad.[1] Perhaps the most important problem was that her peace treaty with Argos, her most powerful rival in the Peloponnese, was soon to expire. The Spartans knew that an alliance of Athens and Argos was a potential threat to their safety. They decided that it was imperative to maintain the peace with Athens at least until they could come to terms with Argos. However, the execution of the terms of the treaty was not going well. The Chalcidians refused to hand Amphipolis over to the Athenians, and the Spartans did not have sufficient control over the area to demand it. As a substitute the Spartans offered a defensive alliance. The Athenians, under the influence of Nicias, agreed to the alliance and handed over to the Spartans the prisoners who has been captured at Sphacteria.

Sparta's most important allies had not joined the Peace of Nicias, and now they seemed to feel deserted by their leader. There now occurs in Thucydides an extraordinary and complex series of negotiations as a number of states scrambled to find the right side, or at least not to be left on the wrong one. Corinth, Mantinea, and Elis, for different reasons, were especially unhappy with Spartan leadership. Athens too was becoming unhappy with Sparta and the progress of the peace. The Spartans had not been able to deliver Amphipolis, and now there was another irritating grievance. Panactum was an Attic fort near the Boeotian border that had been seized by the Boeotians in 422.[2] Its return had been a major Athenian concern that was assured by the terms of the peace treaty.[3] The Boeotians were not eager to give Panactum back, and refused to do so, unless the Spartans joined them in a separate peace treaty. The Spartans agreed to do this, even though it was in direct violation of the Athenian alliance in which neither side was allowed to make a separate treaty without the other party.[4] The Boeotians agreed to return Panactum, and they did, but only after they had dismantled it.

It was as an opponent to Sparta and an advocate of an alliance with Argos that Alcibiades became one of the dominant leaders in Athens. He had rivals. Hyperbolus wanted to be a leader of the people and to inherit Cleon's political influence. Plutarch tells us that Phaeax too was one of Alcibiades' major rivals.[5] We only know of two possible political enterprises in which Phaeax took part. The Athenians sent him to Italy and Sicily on a diplomatic mission in 422, and he may have taken part in the private negotiations that led to the ostracism of Hyperbolus a few years later. It is impossible to draw any conclusions from these incidents about what kind of influence Phaeax might have had, had he not been eclipsed by Alcibiades.[6]

## The Argive Alliance, 420

Alcibiades did, indeed, eclipse all his younger rivals and, with a master stratagem, catapulted himself into a position as the chief rival to Nicias, then enjoying a period of singular pre-eminence. Alcibiades sent a message privately to Argos requesting that she, along with the Eleans and Mantineans, send representatives to Athens for the purpose of making an alliance.[7] Sparta also sent representatives at this time. The Spartan representatives were all men who had an especially good relationship with Athens, including Endius, a man whose family had strong hereditary ties with Alcibiades' family.[8] They spoke to the boule, defending their alliance with Boeotia on the grounds that it was not aimed against Athens and proposing that Athens deliver Pylos into their hands in return for Panactum. They informed the boule that they came with full powers to negotiate any dispute the Athenians thought important. Alcibiades met with the Spartan envoys privately and assured them that he would give them his full support, if they would not mention their full powers when they spoke to the assembly. He promised to return Pylos to Sparta and to settle other matters of concern to them.

The Spartan envoys agreed to Alcibiades' stipulations and, when they spoke in the assembly, they denied that they had come to Athens with full powers to negotiate. Alcibiades then turned on them and denounced them for duplicity and hypocrisy. The assembly was incensed at the Spartans' behaviour and would have negotiated a treaty with Argos immediately had not an earthquake dissuaded them from making any kind of a decision on that day. On the next day, Nicias asked the assembly to send him to Sparta to negotiate. They agreed, but Nicias was unable to accomplish anything substantial on the major issues of Amphipolis, Panactum, or the Boeotian alliance. Alcibiades took advantage of Athenian dissatisfaction and introduced the representatives of Argos, Mantinea, and Elis to the assembly. The four powers agreed to a defensive alliance that was to last for a hundred years and that would require each state to come to the aid of the others in case of attack.

Scholars have found a number of problems with this episode in Thucydides. Their uneasiness is perhaps best summarized by Hatzfeld, who isolated three key difficulties.[9] (1) Why would the Spartans risk dealing with Alcibiades, an inexperienced young man, best known as an opponent of Sparta? (2) Why would the Spartans agree to perjure themselves and deny that they had come to Athens with full powers to negotiate? (3) How is it possible that Endius could resume a close, working relationship with Alcibiades a few years later after having been so badly treated by him on this occasion?

Andrewes saw that the second of these questions was the most difficult one to answer.[10] Plutarch offers a possible solution to this problem.[11] He says that Alcibiades persuaded the envoys that the boule was always polite. The assembly, Alcibiades continued, did not behave with the same restraint, and if it discovered that the Spartans had unlimited powers, it would make impossible demands. The envoys would do better, he concluded, if they pretended that they had to refer back to Sparta in order to make any final settlement.

Andrewes objected to the motivation that Plutarch supplied for this episode for the following reasons.[12] (1) There is other information in this and the following chapter of a questionable nature. (2) The Spartans had nothing substantial to offer. (3) Alcibiades would have to guard the Spartan envoys from contact with Nicias. (4) The Spartans could refer back to Sparta only if they were certain of a good result. None of these arguments disproves Plutarch's explanation. The first point is irrelevant. The second seems to be true, but in what way does it refute the idea that the assembly was less polite than the boule? The third would be true no matter what kind of reason Alcibiades might give the Spartan envoys for reversing the statements that they made to the boule. Andrewes's fourth objection does not seem convincing either. The Spartans may have thought that, in handing over the defortified Panactum, they would be giving in to a major Athenian demand. At any rate, they wanted the return of Pylos, and if reference back to Sparta could facilitate that goal, there is no reason to believe that the delay would hamper Spartan interests.

Plutarch's explanation conforms with common sense. The assembly, being a more public body, would be a more likely place for political grandstanding.[13] Even if it were not the case, it seems probable enough to have convinced the Spartans to hedge their bets. There is no good reason to reject Plutarch's explanation of why the Spartans were willing to reverse their statement and to deny that they had full powers to negotiate.[14]

Hatzfeld's solution to these problems is ingenious, but it has the undesirable ingredient of contradicting the evidence of Thucydides.[15] Hatzfeld emphasizes the idea that the Spartans had really nothing to offer. They either could not or would not give back Amphipolis; they could not refortify Panactum, and they would not abrogate their treaty with the Boeotians. On this point Hatzfeld's reasoning is quite sound. But he goes on to suggest that Alcibiades' 'trick' consisted of exposing the fact that the Spartans had nothing to offer to the assembly. Hatzfeld wants us to believe that Thucydides was wrong about the 'full powers'; that he was led astray because when he returned to Athens in 404 to write his account, he found himself in an atmosphere where the Spartans could do no wrong, and anything that Alcibiades had done was highly suspect. Andrewes has, with some reservations, accepted this view.[16] It seems a drastic solution to a problem that can be more easily explained.[17]

Hatzfeld was right that the key to this problem was the fact that the Spartans had nothing new to offer.[18] They wanted to regain Pylos and to prevent an Argive–Athenian alliance, but they had no substantial concessions to offer. They must have known that Nicias' support was not enough. Then Alcibiades offered his support. Alcibiades was not yet a major leader in Athens, but his name was well known. He came from an aristocratic family, and he had been the ward of Pericles. He had already made it quite clear that he was an opponent to the peace with Sparta and a proponent of an alliance with Argos.[19] With the support of both Nicias and a well-known rival, the Spartans might well have believed that they could gain important concessions without sacrificing anything substantial. With Nicias' support alone, they were likely to gain nothing. The Spartans may have been naïve, but they were not taking a foolish risk. They had everything to gain and nothing much to lose.

There remains the problem of Endius. It is entirely possible that Endius simply found Alcibiades useful eight years later and so decided to ignore his past behaviour.[20] It is also possible that Endius and Alcibiades were in collusion.[21] There is no evidence for this, but it is an attractive theory. But what could have been Endius' motivation for destroying the Spartan mission to Athens? Kebric has an elaborate and fanciful idea that Endius, like Lysander after him, wanted 'to overthrow the hereditary monarchy'.[22] This is speculation on thin air, but in building up his case, Kebric suggests that both Alcibiades and Endius wanted to wreck the peace talks and to precipitate the reopening of the war in order to further their own careers. We know that there was a faction at Sparta that was opposed to the peace.[23] Endius could have been a part, openly or secretly, of this faction. The collapse of the Spartan embassy did not seem to hurt his career, and the reopening of the war may have helped it. At any rate, he did become ephor later, after the war had been officially reopened.

By way of summary, I would like to answer Hatzfeld's reservations and to suggest that Thucydides' account is coherent and complete and can stand without any revisions. (1) The Spartans risked dealing with Alcibiades because they had no hope of gaining any concessions without his co-operation. (2) They followed his suggestion to deny that they had full powers because it sounded logical and because it seemed a painless way to get something (i.e. Pylos or an end to the Argive–Athenian negotiations) for nothing. (3) Endius could work with Alcibiades eight years later because it was politically expedient at the time or because they had already worked together for their mutual benefit.

### Alcibiades' Peloponnesian policy and the battle of Mantinea, 420–418

Early in the sixth book of his *History*, Thucydides gives us a debate on the Sicilian expedition between Alcibiades and Nicias. In that debate Alcibiades makes the following statement.

> Remember that I brought about a coalition of the greatest powers of the Peloponnese, without putting you to any considerable danger or expense, and made the Spartans risk their all on the issue of one day's fighting at Mantinea, and though they were victorious in the battle, they have not even yet quite recovered their confidence.[24]

This statement of his intent contains the characteristics of the kind of policy that we rightly associate with Alcibiades, a policy that includes daring, economy, and diplomacy. As in the episode of the Spartan envoys and in his later plan for the conquest of Sicily,[25] Alcibiades tried to gain as much as possible through negotiation. Only when he had as much ammunition as he could collect, would he attack, and then he would strike suddenly, using the least amount of force necessary to accomplish his goal. This Peloponnesian policy was not ultimately successful, but, as the speech in Thucydides implies, he came close to humiliating Sparta with a single engagement. The Spartans had everything to lose at Mantinea; the Athenians very little. Perhaps if Alcibiades had been allowed to enforce his policy as the general in charge of operations in 418, the outcome would have been different.

The Argive Alliance (also known as the Quadruple Alliance since it included Elis and Mantinea) seemed to bear fruit immediately. The Spartans were not allowed to participate in the Olympic games of 420.[26] That winter the Spartan colony of Heraclea in Trachis was attacked by its neighbours, and in the spring it was taken over by the Boeotians who apparently thought that the Spartans were no longer capable of defending it.[27] Spartan fortunes, which had taken a turn for the worse with the Athenian occupation of Pylos in 425, seemed to continue on a downward path.

In the summer of 419 Alcibiades marched into the Peloponnese with a few Athenian archers and hoplites and with support from Athens' new allies. His route was probably the one Gomme suggested: from Athens to Argos by sea, from Argos to Mantinea and Elis and from there to Patrae.[28] Alcibiades made some unspecified arrangements in connection with the Quadruple Alliance and also persuaded the people of Patrae to build long walls to connect their city with the sea. Plutarch gives us an anecdote in connection with this event. He says that Patrae's neighbours warned them that the Athenians would swallow them up. Alcibiades, hearing this remark, added, 'Perhaps so . . . but you will go slowly, and . . . feet first; whereas Sparta will swallow you head first, and at one gulp.'[29]

Alcibiades intended to build a fort at Rhium on the coast of Achaea opposite Naupactus, the latter having been an Athenian stronghold for many years. With Patrae, Rhium, and Naupactus under her command, Athens could virtually control the entrance to the Corinthian Gulf.[30] Hatzfeld saw that this idea of controlling the Corinthian Gulf had occurred to both Pericles and Cleon.[31] And, like his predecessors, Alcibiades also was unable to accomplish this ambitious project. Forces arrived from Corinth and Sicyon to prevent him from fortifying Rhium. Still,

Alcibiades' expedition to the Peloponnese was important as 'propaganda that advertised the weakness of Sparta and the strength of the new league'.[32]

Alcibiades apparently persuaded the Argives to attack Epidaurus. The pretext was the usual sort of charge used for these occasions, the violation of some minor religious observance. The real motive, says Thucydides, was 'to keep Corinth quiet' and to create a shorter route for Athenian soldiers to reach Argos.[33] Kagan has an attractive theory about Alcibiades' master plan.[34] Alcibiades knew, Kagan surmises, that the fall of Epidaurus would threaten Corinth with attack from both sides, the other side being Patrae or Naupactus. This threat might be enough to scare Corinth out of its alliance with Sparta. Athens and her allies could score a major victory by making Corinth an ally or, at least, a neutral state. Sparta's northern allies, such as Boeotia and Megara, would no longer enjoy easy access to the Peloponnese. And perhaps other Peloponnesian states would follow, abandoning a Sparta whose strength and prestige would continue to decline. Kagan's theory is impossible to prove, but it would go a long way to explain Thucydides' otherwise inexplicable comment about keeping Corinth quiet. It also conforms to the type of strategy Alcibiades favoured, a strategy combining daring, economy, and diplomacy. All these goals could even be obtained, after the conquest of Epidaurus, without a single battle. Kagan, like Hatzfeld, sees Alcibiades' debt to Pericles.

> It is striking that the two actions Alcibiades took in 419 had been undertaken by Pericles at earlier times; indeed, the similarity between the general strategic approaches of each man is marked. We may guess that Alcibiades had studied the career of his guardian closely and rejected not only the ineffective quietism of Nicias but also reckless adventures on land or sea. His plan might or might not work, but it was rational and prudent.[35]

The plan, in fact, did not work. The rest of that summer saw a series of false starts and unresolved conflicts. The Spartans marched to their border in full force under King Agis. Thucydides says that the sacrifices were not favourable and that the Spartans marched home without anyone knowing the aim of the operation.[36] But surely this show of force was a threat aimed at the Argives and their invasion of Epidaurus.[37] The Athenians then called a peace conference at Mantinea. If the purpose of this conference was to involve Corinth in such a way as to pull her away from the Spartan camp, it was a failure. The Corinthian representative quite logically suggested that, if the assembled parties really wanted peace, they had but to withdraw their armies. He went on to insist that a truce was an essential first step toward any further negotiations. The Argives complied with his wishes and withdrew from Epidaurus, apparently hoping for some concessions from Corinth. But nothing came of this peace conference, and the Argives again invaded Epidaurus. The Spartans again marched to their border, and Alcibiades led a thousand Athenian hoplites to the defence of Argos. The Spartans, however, withdrew and so did the Athenians. We can never know what the outcome might have been if a major battle had taken place in the summer of 419, but at least Alcibiades would have been in charge of his own policy. Alcibiades was probably not re-elected general in the spring of 418,[38] and the battle that was fought that summer was in the hands of unsympathetic generals who sent inadequate forces and reinforcements that arrived only after the battle was over.

The parallels with the later Sicilian disaster are obvious and perhaps instructive of the Athenian frame of mind. The Athenian people could not fully support either Alcibiades or Nicias, and the half-hearted compromises that were made failed to execute fully the policy of either man.[39] The battle that almost took place in the summer of 419 scared the Athenians and helped them to realize that Alcibiades' Peloponnesian policy was likely to lead to a full-scale land battle between Athens and Sparta. This explains why Alcibiades was denied the opportunity of exercising the generalship at Mantinea.[40]

During the winter of 418/417 the Spartans sent a garrison by sea to Epidaurus under the command of Agesippidas.[41] The Argives claimed that this entrance into Athenian waters constituted a violation of the Quadruple Alliance.[42] The Argives demanded that the Athenians put a force of Messenians and helots in Pylos to conduct raids against Sparta. Alcibiades persuaded the Athenians to send helots[43] and also to carve an inscription on the pillar that recorded the Spartan peace treaty to the effect that the Spartans did not keep their promises.

Alcibiades' name is not conspicuously present in Thucydides' account of the military manoeuvres in the summer of 418 leading up to the battle of Mantinea, contributing further to the impression that he was not a general at the time. The Spartans did not act until midsummer. They may have waited until the new board of generals took office in Athens.[44] Gomme vigorously denied that there was any evidence for a 'peace-party' in Athens.[45] Yet the mere fact that Nicias was re-elected, and

Alcibiades was probably not re-elected until after the battle suggests a change in the mood of the Athenian people. It may be impossible to prove that Laches and Nicostratus, the generals that the Athenians sent to Argos, were partisans of Nicias, but it is even less likely that they were partisans of Alcibiades.[46] Gomme found it an 'exasperating assumption' that the Spartans would attack after a less militant board took office,[47] but what more could the Spartans ask for than what they actually got, a chance to reassert their military superiority against an army of Athenians and Athenian allies, equal or perhaps inferior in size?[48]

The new board probably represented a shift in public opinion, but not a radical departure from the past. The new generals were not in a position to abandon totally Athens' Peloponnesian allies. There existed in Athens a delicate balance. In between the followers of Nicias and those of Alcibiades, a significant number of Athenians were uncommitted and capable of tipping the scales first in one direction and then in another. This seems a reasonable inference from the events of these years. That is the tragedy of this period of Athenian history, and it led directly to the catastrophic results of the Sicilian expedition. If the Athenians had consistently followed the policy of either Nicias or Alcibiades, they would have been better served than they were in their misguided attempts to accommodate the policies of both men.[49]

King Agis of Sparta led his army and his Arcadian allies against Argos. Other Spartan allies, including Corinth, met at Phlius. Agis avoided immediate combat, and manoeuvred the inferior army of Argives, Mantineans, and Eleans into a position that was both between the two opposing armies and also cut off from Argos. But rather than fight a battle, Agis concluded a four-month truce with two Argive leaders, Thrasylus, a general, and Alciphron, the Spartan proxenos for Argos. This decision proved unpopular with both sides. The Athenians arrived with a thousand hoplites and three hundred cavalry under Laches and Nicostratus, with Alcibiades as ambassador. Alcibiades persuaded the Argives that the truce was not valid since Athens, their ally, had not been a party to it. The allies then marched out and besieged Orchomenus. The people of Orchomenus agreed to surrender and join the alliance. The Athenians, Argives, and Mantineans agreed to attack Tegea next. The Eleans, however, were not happy with this choice and returned home with their forces.[50]

The Spartans, having heard that there was agitation in Tegea to go over to the Athenian side, marched out under an Agis who had gained great unpopularity for his truce with Argos. The Spartans won a decisive victory at Mantinea, a victory that restored their confidence in themselves as well as the confidence of much of the Greek world in the ability of the Spartan army. When the battle was over, three thousand Eleans and a reinforcement of one hundred Athenians arrived too late to save the day. Their intervention earlier might have changed the outcome of the battle. The consequences of the battle were immediate and significant. Argos, whose democracy gave way to an oligarchy, Elis, and Mantinea all abandoned the Athenian alliance and made their peace with Sparta.

The battle of Mantinea had not been a victory for Alcibiades, but neither was it an event of which his opponents could be proud. A larger and more punctual response under the leadership of Alcibiades might have led to a different outcome. Thucydides tells us very little about the history of Greece between the battle of Mantinea and the launching of the Sicilian expedition, but we are left with the definite impression that the frantic pace of the preceding two years dwindled to a virtual standstill. The democrats eventually regained power in Argos, but the pursuit of Peloponnesian allies had temporarily lost favour in Athens. It is tempting to see the period as a stalemate between the followers of Alcibiades and those of Nicias, neither side strong enough to dominate Athenian policy.[51] The Athenians had a remedy for this kind of stalemate, the institution of ostracism.

## The ostracism of Hyperbolus

The ostracism of Hyperbolus was traditionally thought to have occurred in the year 417 and to have been a result of the stalemate in Athenian politics after the battle of Mantinea that had been achieved as a result of the rivalry of Nicias and Alcibiades[52]. The traditional view has been challenged in recent years. The date was derived from a combination of Thucydides[53], who said that Hyperbolus was assassinated in Samos in 411, and a fragment of Theopompus[54] that implied that it had been six years since Hyperbolus was ostracized. Woodhead[55] suggested that a decree[56] to which Hyperbolus had added an amendment may have been passed late in 418/417, too late for Hyperbolus to have been ostracized in the spring of 417. This hypothesis was accepted by McGregor.[57] Raubitschek sought to move the date down to 415 and to place the incident within the context of the debate on the Sicilian expedition.[58] His argument is not convincing and has found little support.[59] Fuqua came up with a happy compromise.[60] He showed that, by inclusive reckoning, Theopompus could have counted back from the Athenian year 412/411 and arrived at the year 417/416, thus placing the ostracism in 416. Unless archaeology turns up new evidence, we cannot be certain of the date, for neither Woodhead's decree nor the Theopompus fragment offers certain evidence. But in the light of the present controversy, the year 416 seems both the most likely date for the ostracism of Hyperbolus and a reasonable, working compromise.[61]

However, if we do accept the date 416, it is difficult to place the ostracism within the context of either the battle of Mantinea or the Sicilian expedition. Thucydides tells us very little about the events of this year. He tells us only the bare fact that Hyperbolus was ostracized, and even this information comes belatedly at the time of Hyperbolus' assassination in 411.[62] We must go to Plutarch, who tells it three times, for the story of the ostracism. In his *Aristides* Plutarch says that the people voted for an ostracism, and that Nicias and Alcibiades were the obvious choices.[63] Nicias and Alcibiades pooled their resources and, for their mutual benefit, caused the vote to fall on Hyperbolus. Nicias and Alcibiades then would seem to be the conspirators, and Hyperbolus merely the victim. In the *Nicias* Hyperbolus initiated the movement in the hope of bolstering his own career by becoming the major rival of whichever leader, Nicias or Alcibiades, was left after his opponent had been ostracized.[64] Nicias and Alcibiades then came to an agreement, in self-defence, and rallied their supporters to vote against Hyperbolus. In the *Nicias* Plutarch mentions that Theophrastus, Aristotle's successor, told the story differently. According to Theophrastus it was Alcibiades and Phaeax, not Nicias, who joined forces to gain the ostracism of Hyperbolus. Plutarch dismissed the story and so have most subsequent commentators. Indeed, it does not make much sense. Why would Alcibiades make such an effort to rid himself of a man whose presence was no great threat to him, but whose removal was to create, as we shall see, a potent hostility against him? In the *Alcibiades* Plutarch tells the story as he did in the *Nicias* with only a slight variation.[65] Here, Phaeax was also a candidate for ostracism, and Plutarch does not dismiss quite so emphatically the idea that Alcibiades and Phaeax collaborated against Hyperbolus.

Ostracism, a device by which a man had to leave Athens for ten years but without loss of property and with only temporary loss of citizenship, was neither frivolous nor was it really a disgrace. It was reserved for the most important leaders of the state. It arose from the Athenians' distaste for tyrants, and it served a useful purpose. It was used to remove any leader whose popularity threatened the freedom of the people. In the ninth decade of the fifth century, ostracism could have been used as an effective tool of Athenian democracy. The rivalry of Alcibiades and Nicias had created an impasse. Athens would have been more fortunate if either Alcibiades or Nicias had been ostracized.[66] The defeat at Mantinea had been an example of what Athens could expect if she tried to walk the thin line between the very different policies of these two leaders. The disaster in Sicily was the ultimate monument to the tragic folly of trying to appease two men who led in opposite directions. We can only guess at the machinations by which Alcibiades and Nicias, the two primary targets, avoided ostracism. Plutarch thought that the misuse of ostracism on an unworthy victim and for the unworthy purpose of protecting the intended victims is what led the Athenians never to employ the device again. He quoted Plato the comic poet:

> The man deserved the fate, deny who can:
> Yes, but the fate did not deserve the man.[67]

Each year the assembly voted, in the sixth prytany, whether to have an ostracism. No ostracism had been held in Athens, of which we have any knowledge, since 443. Who was behind the movement to hold one in 416? It is not enough to say, as Plutarch does,[68] that the people decided to hold an ostracism. Ostracisms were not regularly held without issues, and these issues were not decided without the support or opposition of powerful leaders. Even if the vote for ostracism represented some sort of popular ground swell, the major leaders of Athens would have taken part in the discussions and machinations. Is it likely that Hyperbolus would have the necessary influence to precipitate an ostracism against the combined supporters of Nicias and Alcibiades? It is a much more likely scenario that one of the major figures was trying to get rid of his opponent and Alcibiades, given his penchant for the devious, is the more likely candidate.

Grote thought that the followers of Nicias would be more likely to inaugurate the ostracism, because Alcibiades 'was the person most likely to be reputed dangerous.'[69] This is possible, but Nicias, a man noted for his caution and reserve, does not seem the kind of person who would relish secret schemes and plots. Alcibiades, on the other hand, gloried in conflict and intrigue. If Alcibiades once set his mind to the ostracism of

Nicias, he would need allies, and he would certainly seek the aid of both Phaeax and Hyperbolus. There was a certain amount of time, about two months, between the vote to hold an ostracism and the actual vote on the ostracism.[70] Alcibiades may have found his support slipping and made a last-minute arrangement with Nicias and Phaeax to deflect the votes of their followers to Hyperbolus. This speculative scenario would explain the intense bitterness that the followers of Hyperbolus, under the leadership of Androcles, felt for Alcibiades from that day onwards.[71]

If we place the ostracism in the year 416, it is possible to see it in a very different light than if we place it in the year 417. Although Alcibiades had not been totally disgraced by the battle of Mantinea, since he had not been allowed to take part in the battle in a military capacity, he was definitely in a vulnerable position. His Peloponnesian policy had borne no fruit and was now in virtual collapse. Sparta seemed stronger than ever and in full control of the Peloponnese.

It is possible that the political climate was quite different in Athens only a year later. Nicias had had a chance to implement his policy. He had tried to recover Amphipolis in the summer of 417 and failed.[72] The failure was primarily due to the duplicity of King Perdiccas of Macedonia, but the collapse of the expedition could not help but reflect badly on Nicias. In the meantime the Argive democrats regained control of their city. They abandoned their treaty with Sparta, made a new treaty with Athens, and began to build walls to the sea so that they could receive aid from the Athenians if they were besieged by the Spartans.[73] Plutarch credits Alcibiades with persuading the Argives to build the walls and adds that he brought stone-masons and carpenters with him from Athens to work on the walls.[74] If, as has been suggested, the vote took place at this juncture, Nicias would have been the party in disgrace, and Alcibiades would have been at the height of his popularity.[75]

In summary, I would like to suggest the following scenario concerning the ostracism of Hyperbolus. Hyperbolus himself was not influential enough to have been the driving force behind this movement. Alcibiades, whether he initiated the proceedings or not, would have taken part. He would have tried to gather as many allies as possible, and he might initially have solicited the support of Phaeax and Hyperbolus against Nicias. This could explain how Phaeax's name became involved in the tradition. It is also possible that Alcibiades believed, at the last minute, that he was going to lose and so shifted his support to Nicias, and together they instructed their followers to deflect the ostracism to

Hyperbolus. This could explain why the followers of Hyperbolus, under the leadership of Androcles, felt such special bitterness toward Alcibiades. If Alcibiades did prevent the people from choosing between him and Nicias, it was a major mistake both for him and for Athens. Alcibiades ensured that Athens would continue to suffer divided and indecisive leadership. He had ensured for himself the enmity of a portion of the radical democrats who would no longer trust him, and who would wait for an opportunity to exact their revenge.

## Melos and the Olympics of 416

The new Athenian–Argive alliance may have bolstered Alcibiades' reputation temporarily, but it had very little long-range effect. The Spartans marched on Argos in the winter of 417/416. They tore down the long walls that Alcibiades had been assisting the Argives in building, and they massacred the inhabitants of the Argive town of Hysia.[76]

This last action may have influenced the Athenians in their seemingly unwarranted attack on the neutral island of Melos in the following summer. Melos, a Spartan colony and ally, was one of the few islands of any significant size left in the Aegean that had not become a part of the Athenian Empire. In the summer of 416 the Athenians demanded, not for the first time,[77] that the Melians become a member of their empire. The Athenians besieged the island until they won an unconditional surrender the following winter. The Athenians killed all the men of military age and sold the women and children into slavery.

The eloquence of Thucydides ensured that this brutal incident has become one of the best-known events in Greek history. In the 'Melian Dialogue'[78] he has left us an indelible portrait of the nameless and merciless Athenian negotiators who argue that the strong do what they can and that the weak must submit. In 405, when the Athenians had lost the war, and they awaited the victorious Spartans, it was said that they lay awake fearing that they might receive the same fate that they themselves had decreed against the Melians.[79] In later times the massacre of the Melians became a standard accusation made against the brutality of Athenian imperialism.[80]

Plutarch and [Andocides], who may or may not represent separate traditions,[81] both ascribe responsibility, in one way or another, to Alcibiades for the policy of Athens toward Melos.[82] There are reasons for doubting this. It is not the sort of campaign Alcibiades normally championed. It seems more like the kind of small operation, directed at tightening up the defences of the present empire, usually associated with Nicias, rather than the daring attacks on major targets that we normally associate with Alcibiades. Nicias had led an earlier expedition against Melos,[83] and there is some evidence, although hardly convincing evidence, that he was present at the final reduction of Melos.[84]

At the time that the Melian expedition was launched, Alcibiades was taking part in a campaign against the pro-Spartan citizens of Argos,[85] an activity that was surely of greater importance to him than the relatively unimportant island of Melos. It is a sad comment on the mental attitude of the Athenians at this stage of a long and brutal war, but the truth is probably that Melos was not even a controversial issue at the time.[86] Melos had been assessed for tribute as early as 425,[87] which means, in a sense, that the Athenians already considered the island as a part of their empire. The expedition was entrusted to relatively minor generals. After the Spartan treatment of Plataea and Hysia and the Athenian treatment of Scione,[88] the policy of annihilation had become commonplace.

There is one anecdote of doubtful veracity concerning Alcibiades and the aftermath of the siege of Melos. [Andocides] says that Alcibiades purchased a Melian woman who had been sold into slavery and had a son by her.[89] This document that is listed as number four among the speeches of Andocides is now universally rejected as a work by that orator, and most historians believe it was written long after the events it describes.[90] But it purports to be a speech that was given in the assembly in 415 shortly before the sailing of the Athenian expedition to Sicily. The speaker asserts that Alcibiades purchased a slave and that since that time he has had a son by her. This is impossible chronologically, assuming that he bought the slave after the fall of Melos, because Melos fell in the winter of 416/415 and this speech would have to have been delivered in the spring or early summer of 415. However, it is not impossible that Alcibiades bought a Melian slave and had a son by her,[91] a son who was born, perhaps, after his father had sailed off to Sicily. This event, like others in the speech, was only imperfectly remembered or researched by the author of [Andocides] 4.

In the Olympic games of 416 Alcibiades entered seven chariot teams and won the first, second, and fourth places.[92] No private citizen had ever entered this many teams in the games before, and his accomplishments represented to Plutarch 'all that ambition can aspire to in this field'.[93] Alcibiades celebrated his victory on a lavish scale. The people of Ephesus erected a huge tent for him, considerably larger than the official Athenian headquarters. The Chians supplied him with feed for his horses and sacrificial animals. The people of Lesbos supplied wine and other items necessary for a grandiose celebration.[94] Alcibiades took pride in all this, and he later boasted, according to Thucydides, that he brought glory to Athens at a time when her reputation was suffering.[95] The Greek world came to believe that Athens was even greater than it really was, he claimed, as a result of his magnificent display.

This magnificent display may have been still another aspect of the rivalry between Alcibiades and Nicias. Nicias too was capable of lavish public expenditure although his spectacles were characteristically of a more pious nature. In 417 Nicias had made a great impression on his countrymen with his extravagant reorganization of the ceremonies to Apollo at Delos. He built a bridge of boats between the nearby island of Rheneia and Delos and led over it a procession of worshippers, chanting a hymn to the god. Nicias provided banquets, choral contests, and sacrifices, and he dedicated an estate worth 10,000 drachmas to Apollo.[96] Alcibiades may have thought that he had to find an equally flamboyant way of gaining public attention.

The only sour note in Alcibiades' victory celebration at Olympia related to his alleged misappropriation of one of the seven chariot teams. Diomedes was an Athenian and a friend of Alcibiades who, according to Plutarch, asked Alcibiades to purchase a team of horses for him from the city of Argos.[97] Alcibiades purchased the team from Argos, a city with which he had an enormous amount of influence, but then he entered it at Olympia as one of his own. This case eventually came to court, but by the time it did, both the principals had changed. Isocrates wrote a speech (*c.*396) for Alcibiades' son, Alcibiades IV, to deliver in his own defence in a suit that was brought against him by Teisias for the theft of a team of racehorses. Why did this case take twenty years to come to court and why was Teisias, and not Diomedes, the plaintiff? We shall probably never know the answers to these questions since the first part of the speech, the part that would have explained these matters, is lost. Davies, following the hypothesis of Münsterberg, suggested that Teisias was the friend of Alcibiades who tried to buy the racehorses from Argos.[98] According to Davies and Münsterberg, [Andocides], Diodorus, and Plutarch all borrowed from Ephorus and mis-understood a mythological allusion to Heracles who captured the man-eating mares of Diomedes, king of Thrace. This is possible, but Hatzfeld's suggestion that Teisias and Diomedes were partners and that Diomedes died before the case came to court is a more likely solution to the problem.[99] One reason why the case did not come to court earlier is that Alcibiades did not spend much of the remaining eleven years of his life in Athens. After he left Athens in 415 as a leader of the great Sicilian expedition, he returned home but once and then only briefly.

# Chapter four

# Sicily and defection

## Athens and the West

Athens had long been interested in the Greek cities of Sicily and southern Italy. Themistocles named one of his daughters Italia and another Sybaris, and he was associated in other ways with a western policy.[1] The Athenians may have concluded an alliance with Segesta (or Egesta) as early as 458/457.[2] Probably with the encouragement of Pericles,[3] they also made alliances with Rhegion and Leontini.[4]

The Athenians maintained a presence in Sicily for three years during the Archidamian War (427–424).[5] The ostensible reason for the expedition was to defend Athens' ally, Leontini, against the encroachments of Syracuse, Sicily's most powerful state.[6] This operation was ultimately unproductive, but at one time or another Athens had found support from a sizeable coalition including Rhegion, the Italian city that was closest to Sicily, Messana, Camarina, Catana, and Naxos as well as a large portion of the Sicel or native population. These cities, with the exception of Messana, whose forced co-operation had been brief and unexpected, were the traditional enemies of Syracuse. Rhegion, Naxos, Leontini, and Catana were all Chalcidian (hence Ionian) cities that maintained a hereditary enmity toward Dorian Syracuse. Camarina, although a Syracusan colony, was a perennial opponent of her mother-city and had twice been invaded by her.

This Athenian operation failed because it had no clearly defined goal and because it was subordinated to the more important campaign at Pylos. Eurymedon and Sophocles, who had been sent with reinforcements for Sicily, were understandably detained at Pylos. The capture of Spartan prisoners on Sphacteria was a brilliant victory for the Athenians, but it probably ensured Athenian defeat in Sicily. By the time

53

Eurymedon and Sophocles reached Sicily, any momentum for victory there had been lost. In 424 the Sicilians met at the Congress of Gela to discuss ways to bring peace to the island. The Syracusan Hermocrates, according to Thucydides, made an impressive speech in which he exhorted the assembled delegates to settle Sicilian differences among themselves and to avoid calling in outside powers.[7] The delegates agreed, and the result of the Congress of Gela was, in effect, to exclude Athens from any involvement in the west.

Athens' ally, Leontini, continued to have problems. The democrats there were planning to redistribute the land, but the aristocracy learned of their plans and called in the Syracusans, who drove the democrats out of the city. The aristocrats destroyed and abandoned Leontini and went to live in Syracuse. Some of them became dissatisfied with the Syracusans, returned home to what was left of Leontini, and made peace with most of the democrats. Together the reunited Leontines began a fight to resurrect their homeland.

In 422 Athens sent Phaeax, whose role as one of Alcibiades' rivals and as one of the participants in the ostracism of Hyperbolus was discussed in Chapter Three, to Sicily and Italy to defend the democrats of Leontini and to look for other allies who might be unhappy with the aggressive behaviour of Syracuse.[8] Although Phaeax achieved nothing of lasting importance, he did discover several other western states that were unhappy with Syracuse and the philosophy of the Congress of Gela. This embassy reveals Athens' continuing interest in the west. It may have stimulated the Segestans six years later, when they were being besieged by their neighbours, to apply to Athens for help.

## The debate on the Sicilian expedition

Alcibiades, after the ostracism of Hyperbolus in 416 (see pp. 45–9),[9] became the leading advocate of a western expedition. His later plans for the expedition reveal an intimate knowledge of Sicily and which states might be exploited as allies.[10] Indeed, Athens, as the preceding section should suggest, had had a long and persistent relationship with the west. Thucydides' statement[11] that Athens was largely ignorant of the size and population of Sicily is misleading. The Athenians had contemplated a western expedition for a long time, and their enthusiasm for Sicily was not an instance of mass hysteria. However, when the Segestan envoys came to Athens in the winter of 416/415 they found an unusually receptive audience. The Athenians had been nominally at peace since 421, and a great many young men were eager for adventure.[12] Athens' Aegean empire was secure, but the attempts to make inroads into the Peloponnese and to recover lost allies in the north had proved futile. It was neither surprising then nor illogical that Athens should turn to the west.

Segesta was a non-Greek city in western Sicily. She went to war with her neighbour, the Greek city of Selinus, over disputed territory and disagreements concerning marriage rights. The Selinuntines defeated the Segestans in battle and then persuaded the Syracusans to join them in a siege of Segesta by land and sea. The Segestans and, according to Diodorus,[13] the still homeless Leontines sent to Athens for help in 416/415. The Segestans argued, probably with the support of Alcibiades, that if the Syracusans were allowed to continue unchecked, they would acquire complete control of Sicily and would then come to the aid of the Spartans against Athens. The Athenians voted to send a delegation to investigate the wealth of the Segestans and the progress of their war against Selinus. This decision was probably a compromise of the sort that had now become all too familiar between the supporters of Alcibiades, who favoured an expedition, and those of Nicias, who opposed it.

The Segestans deceived the Athenian envoys with an elaborate show of wealth.[14] They gathered all the silver and gold vessels at their disposal[15] and displayed them at every banquet, as if each host owned a private fortune. The hoax worked, and the Athenians came home in the spring of 415 telling stories of the enormous wealth that existed in Sicily. The assembly voted to send sixty ships to Sicily under the joint command of Alcibiades, Nicias, and Lamachus.[16]

Another assembly was held several days later to discuss the possibility of increasing the supplies for the expedition. It was on this occasion, according to Thucydides, that the Athenians held a major discussion of the Sicilian policy.[17] These speeches are not verbatim accounts of what was said, but they must reflect some of the issues that were vital to the Athenians at the time. The circumstances of this discussion recall the Mytilenian Debate in that the assembly had already made a decision, and then met later to reconsider it. Only this time they did not change their minds.

Nicias said that, although he had nothing to lose from it personally, he thought that the expedition was bad policy – just as in the Mytilenian Debate, there is no discussion of morality; the only concern is what is best for Athens. Nicias, in the speech that Thucydides gives him, reminded the Athenians that they had only recently overcome the ill effects of the plague and the Archidamian War. The Spartans and the Boeotians would be willing to resume the war if the Athenians wandered too far from home. Now was the time, Nicias continued, to consolidate the empire they already had rather than to try to build a new one. Sicily, even if defeated, could not be controlled; it was too far away. Nicias then attacked Alcibiades personally, although not by name. He said that his opponent only wanted the expedition for selfish reasons: to further his political career and to enhance his private fortune. Nicias called upon the older men to forestall this reckless movement of the younger generation.

Thucydides next characterizes Alcibiades in a way that at first seems to support Nicias' view but then suggests a very different evaluation altogether.[18] He says that Alcibiades was lawless and extravagant. The people turned away from him and followed other, lesser leaders, and for this reason the city came to ruin. This is a subtle point. Alcibiades does not escape blame, but the major fault seems to lie with the people who turned away from the best possible leader that Athens had at the time. Thucydides foreshadowed this idea much earlier in his *History*. In condemning the successors of Pericles, he said that the Sicilian disaster was a mistake, not in design, but in execution. It came to ruin because the people at home did not support the expedition properly. This can only mean the recall of Alcibiades, for in every other way the expedition was lavishly supported.[19]

Thucydides allows Alcibiades a chance to answer Nicias.[20] Alcibiades claimed that his extravagances, especially his victories at Olympia, had brought honour and prestige to Athens. He boasted of his exploits in the Peloponnese. Alcibiades wisely refrained from attacking Nicias, but rather asked the assembly to send both men on the expedition: he himself because he was in the vigour of his youth, and Nicias, because he had a reputation for good luck. He thought that Sicily was not a great power because the individual states lacked civic cohesion and would not act consistently as states or as alliances. Their hoplites were not as numerous as was thought.

The Athenians could easily make allies in Sicily, Alcibiades continued, if they offered attractive propositions to the right people. The Sicilian states, according to Alcibiades' informants, were divided by civil strife which would make the Athenians' task easier. The Athenians could also depend on the non-Hellenic states, who hated the Syracusans and would be willing to join a coalition against them. These ideas are perfectly consistent with Alcibiades' plans as outlined by Thucydides later in his *History* when the three generals discuss strategy in Italy.[21]

Alcibiades insisted that Athens should heed the requests of Segesta. That is how she had built an empire in the past. That is how all empires are made: by coming to the aid of anyone who asks for it. Alcibiades ended the speech on a Periclean note.[22] He exhorted the city to greatness. Athens was not the kind of state, he said, that could afford to be idle. She must always be achieving new goals and new greatness or she would become stagnant and decay.

After more speeches by Segestans and Leontine exiles, Nicias, according to Thucydides,[23] tried to scare the Athenians out of the expedition by exaggerating the resources that would be necessary for it. He said that the Athenians would be setting out against states that were strong and not unhappy with their way of life. There were many Greek cities on the island, he continued, but only Naxos and Catana would be likely to join them against Syracuse. Their opponents had certain advantages over the Athenians, especially in the number of their horses and in the fact that they would be in control of their own grain supplies. Nicias warned the assembly that they would need a large army of infantry, archers, and slingers. They would need to take their own grain and their own bakers, he suggested, predicting accurately that the Segestans would not provide the great wealth that they had promised.[24]

Nicias' purpose in this speech was to dissuade the Athenians from the expedition, but it had a decidedly different result. The effect of the speech was to consolidate the great majority of Athenians behind the project with an exaggerated sense of enthusiasm. They voted that the three generals should have full powers to arrange as large an expedition as they thought appropriate. Athens became intoxicated with the idea. The city became obsessed with the preparations for the campaign.

According to Thucydides, the few who were actually against it kept quiet for fear of being thought disloyal.[25] Plutarch says that Socrates was an exception to that general rule.[26] He declared his concern to a number of people that no good would come to Athens from this expedition. It is impossible to know whether Alcibiades and Socrates had remained friends until this time, but this issue would certainly have created a distance if not a bitterness in their relationship. Plutarch also tells a curious story about Meton the astronomer.[27] Meton was convinced that this adventure was doomed to failure. In order to avoid going on the expedition he burned down his own house to prove that he was insane. In another version of the story Meton burned down his house secretly in the middle of the night, and the next day he appealed to the people, in the light of his great misfortune, to spare his son from the expedition.

Plutarch, as he often does in his narration of a momentous event, provides us with a collection of signs and portents that were said to have preceded the sailing of the expedition.[28] However, in this case he implies that there was a deliberate propaganda war. Alcibiades, at least, was able to counter pessimistic oracles with his own, more optimistic ones. One portent that was probably not invented[29] was the celebration of the Adonia shortly before the sailing of the expedition.[30] The women mourned the dead Adonis and carried images of him attired for a ritual funeral. The sight of these women mourning publicly and carrying around little statues of dead youths was disturbing to the superstitious. But these other portents were rendered insignificant in the wake of an event that shocked all Athens.

## The mutilation of the herms and the profanation of the Mysteries

One morning before the expedition sailed, the Athenians awoke to find that most of the herms in the city had been mutilated.[31] The herm was a stone sculpture at the head of a pillar, often ornamented with an erect phallus, that stood before both temples and private homes. The deed was considered sacrilegious since the statue represented the god Hermes. Thucydides[32] says that their faces were mutilated, but it is probable that their phalli were knocked off as well.[33] The Athenian people offered rewards for the perpetrators and immunity to anyone who could give information about this or any other sacrilege that had occurred in the city.[34] They set up a commission to investigate the matter that included Diognetus, Nicias' brother, and two men, Pisander and Charicles, who were considered democrats at the time, but who were later associated with the oligarchs.[35] Androcles may have been a member of the commission.[36] The ancient sources do not name him, but they do note his active participation in the proceedings and his enthusiastic efforts to convict Alcibiades of wrongdoing.[37]

The first evidence that was made public had nothing to do with the herms. The slave Andromachus testified to the assembly that he had been present at the house of Pulytion when Alcibiades and others had performed a mock celebration of the Eleusinian Mysteries.[38] Androcles and other enemies of Alcibiades exploited the issue, inflamed the public against Alcibiades and sought to confuse the two incidents,[39] but the mutilation of the herms was probably not related to the profanation of the Mysteries.[40] Most historians have found Alcibiades guilty of profaning the Mysteries but innocent of mutilating the herms, and, in all probability, this is an accurate assessment.[41]

There were three other witnesses who came forth to give testimony on the profanation of the Mysteries.[42] What is not always fully appreciated is the fact that each of these testimonies represented a separate occasion. Andromachus described an enactment of the Mysteries at Pulytion's house. Agariste described a similar celebration at Charmides' house. The slave Lydus testified to a profanation that took place at the house of his master Pherecles of Themacus. The metic Teucrus did not reveal the name of the person at whose house the sacrilege took place, but we can tell from the list of those present that it was a separate gathering from any of the others mentioned. Further, the formal impeachment of Alcibiades lists a fifth occasion at Alcibiades' own house.[43] If these reports can be trusted, and there is no reason to reject them as they must have been a matter of public record, the Mysteries were profaned not once but repeatedly. Alcibiades was reported present at three of these five incidents. Given the wildness of his character, it seems probable that he was involved.

What was the purpose of these sacrileges? These profanations of the Mysteries were probably never meant as a serious threat to either government or religion. They were performed in private homes by people who had neither the intent nor the desire that these ceremonies be brought to the public's attention.[44] They were probably meant as parlour games[45] or, at worst, as initiation ceremonies for a club.[46]

After the first accusation was made by the slave Andromachus, Alcibiades sought to prove his innocence and requested an immediate trial. He asked the assembly not to send him out as a leader of the Sicilian expedition under the suspicion of a capital charge. He begged them either to clear his name first or to sentence him to death if he were found guilty. His enemies knew that he would probably be acquitted if he were tried immediately, and so they worked to postpone his trial until after the fleet had sailed.[47] Alcibiades' opponents produced speakers who persuaded the assembly that the fleet should sail immediately and that this incident should not delay its departure.[48] Alcibiades had been outmanoeuvred, and he had no choice but to comply with the wishes of the assembly and to set sail for Sicily.

Circumstantial evidence, which argues that Alcibiades was

guilty of profaning the Mysteries, argues equally against his participation in the mutilation of the herms. The latter action, unlike the former, was a public act. It is highly doubtful that Alcibiades would be involved in such a stunt on the eve of the sailing of the expedition that he had worked so hard to create. There are some historians who think that the herms were mutilated by revellers engaged in a malicious prank.[49] If so, the revellers would have had to have been unusually well organized and industrious to carry out such a difficult and enterprising work of destruction. Most historians agree that the job was done deliberately and probably by people whose object it was to prevent the sailing of the expedition. If this was the motive of the perpetrators, then the most likely suspects are the friends of Nicias,[50] those Athenians who were oligarchic in sympathy,[51] or the Corinthians.[52] The opposition of Nicias and his friends is well known. The potential oligarchs presumably did not desire the expedition for fear that it would strengthen the democracy. The Corinthians might perpetrate such an act in order to protect Syracuse, their colony and ally.

J.L. Marr has questioned this motive.[53] He says that there was no reason to believe that the mutilation of the herms would cause the Athenians to stop the expedition. Support for it was too strong, and cancellation was never even discussed after the mutilation had occurred. What, in fact, did the Greeks do when a bad omen suggested to them that their plans had not found divine favour? In 420 the Athenians were on the verge of concluding a treaty with Argos when an earthquake occurred.[54] The treaty was delayed, but later it was concluded. The omen was a sign to delay the action, but apparently not to forgo it altogether. In the winter of 413/412 the Spartans, usually considered more superstitious than the Athenians, voted to send a naval force to the rebelling Chians when another earthquake occurred.[55] The Spartans sent the expedition anyway, but they sent a different number of ships and elected a different commanding officer.[56]

Grote believed that there were two motives behind the mutilation of the herms: to frustrate the launching of the expedition and to ruin Alcibiades.[57] It is possible that the purpose of the herm episode was not to prevent the expedition but simply to bring about an investigation that would reveal scandalous information about Alcibiades. If this was the motive, then the name of Androcles must be added to the list of suspects. He was, according to Thucydides, the man who was largely responsible for the recalling of Alcibiades.[58]

Andocides named the people responsible for the mutilation of the herms.[59] In return for this information he gained freedom for himself, his father, and a number of other relatives. This reason alone is enough to make one question the veracity of his testimony. Andocides had everything to gain and little to lose by his confession. The fact that he named primarily people already denounced is also suspicious. However, we cannot dismiss his information totally for it seems to have been convincing enough to force an admission of perjury from Diocleides, the man whose testimony had put Andocides and members of his family in prison. If Andocides' information is credible, then the oligarchs would appear to have been involved. Although it cannot be proved that Andocides' hetaireia held oligarchic sympathies, there is strong circumstantial evidence to suggest it.[60]

In summary, I believe that Alcibiades was guilty of profaning the Mysteries.[61] In the cold light of day, this sacrilege may appear very serious, but I think it was never meant to reach the light of day, and it was no more than a joke in poor taste. Alcibiades was probably innocent of mutilating the herms. In spite of the exhaustive efforts of his enemies, he was never, as far as we know, formally charged with this crime. The motivation of those who were guilty of this action is far from certain. The perpetrators of the act may have performed it as a secret 'pledge' to bind themselves closer together,[62] but toward what further goal?

The friends of Nicias are the least likely suspects. Nicias himself, if his character was anything like as pious and superstitious as it has been portrayed, would never sanction such a sacrilege. His followers were the loyal opposition and the backbone of the Athenian establishment. They do not seem likely candidates for such a desperate act. Neither does it seem likely that the Corinthians would have had the means or opportunity to perform such a deed without causing notice.[63] If the perpetrators were Athenians who had been bribed by the Corinthians, this surely would have come to light in the intense investigation that followed. This leaves the oligarchs and the radical democrats, those who had followed Hyperbolus and were now probably under the influence of Androcles. It is not impossible that they could have worked in tandem. If Alcibiades and Nicias could band together against Hyperbolus, then it is possible that Androcles and the hetaireia of Andocides could work together for the expulsion of Alcibiades.

The usual motive ascribed to the mutilation, i.e. to stop the expedition, needs to be reconsidered. Neither the radical democrats nor the oligarchs were likely to prosper by preventing the expedition. The radical democrats thrived upon the benefits of empire; Cleon and Hyperbolus had both been associated with policies that were designed to expand the empire (se pp. 15–17). The oligarchs were not likely to come to power with the fleet in port. They never would have come to power in 411 if the fleet had not been away. Both groups, however, could hope to benefit by Alcibiades' absence. Both groups stood a better chance of coming to power in the absence of Athens' most charismatic leader. We cannot know if the two groups worked together or if one or the other worked alone, but the radical democrats (or their demagogic leaders) and the oligarchs remain the most likely suspects in the mutilation of the herms. We know little of the domestic affairs of Athens for the next few years, but Androcles certainly gained influence in the vacuum of power created during and after the Sicilian expedition. He probably sought to be a popular leader on the model of Cleon. If, as seems possible, Androcles gained a position of leadership through the removal of Alcibiades, his endeavours were successful, but his victory was short-lived.

## Alcibiades in the west

The Athenian fleet left for Sicily in the summer of 415. Almost the entire population of the city went down to the Piraeus to see it off. Thucydides calls it the most expensive and the best looking force that a single Greek city had ever mounted up until that time.[64] They sailed to Corcyra where their allies were assembling. From Corcyra the fleet sailed to southern Italy where they found the inhabitants unfriendly.[65] They assembled at Rhegion, the old Athenian ally, whose location was conveniently close to Sicily. The Athenians found the people of Rhegion unwilling to join them in their proposed mission of aiding the people of Leontini. It may be that the western Greeks were intimidated by the sheer size of the Athenian expedition.[66] Also at this time the Athenians learned from a party that they had sent ahead of the Segestans' deception: they did not have the kind of wealth that they had pretended to have.

The bad news from Segesta and the coolness of the Italian cities led the Athenian generals to reconsider their strategy. Thucydides allows each general to set forth a plan of action, each of which is characteristic of the man.[67] Nicias suggested that they first sail to the western part of Sicily and try to obtain the promised money from Segesta. If this failed (as was almost certain), the expedition should settle matters between Segesta and Selinus, sail around the island in order to impress the Sicilians with Athenian might, and then go home. If, in the unlikely possibility that they should find a quick and easy way to settle the dispute between Syracuse and the Leontines, then they, in Nicias' view, should do so.

Alcibiades' plan stressed the gathering of allies first. He wanted to send heralds to all the Sicilian cities except Syracuse and Selinus. He thought the Athenians should seek the support of the Sicels, and he stressed the strategic importance of Messana. After they had gathered as many allies as possible, they should attack Syracuse and Selinus unless they could come to terms first without fighting. Lamachus' plan was simple. He advised that they should attack Syracuse immediately while the enemy was still unprepared and her fear of the Athenian expedition was at its peak.

Lamachus' plan has been considered the best of the three by many historians,[68] indeed, Thucydides' narrative itself seems to endorse this strategy.[69] It may be that an immediate attack on Syracuse would have led to a military victory. But Athens could not have held the island of Sicily for long without allies. An immediate attack on Syracuse might have galvanized the whole of Sicily and Magna Graecia against Athens. Alcibiades' plan was to collect again all the allies that Athens had attracted before the Congress of Gela. He was planning for the future, and his strategy was both sound and economical.[70]

Alcibiades' plan here seems modest both in terms of the motives ascribed to him earlier by Thucydides[71] and in terms of what he is reported to have told the Spartans later.[72] During the debate with Nicias, Thucydides reported that Alcibiades wanted to conquer Sicily and Carthage. Thucydides has Alcibiades tell the Spartans that the Athenians wanted to conquer not only Sicily and Carthage but also southern Italy and the Peloponnese[73] and, in fact, become 'masters of the entire Greek world'. This idea has been exaggerated, in my view, and glamorized with the title the 'Grand Design'. No doubt, Athens, if she had been successful in Sicily, would have eventually gone on to expand her influence in the Mediterranean. The idea of an expanded Athenian empire is not difficult to imagine. But there is no real evidence for the sort of secret and sinister campaign that is sometimes implied by use of the phrase, the 'Grand Design'.[74] If Alcibiades' speech in Thucydides resembles the one that he actually gave to the Spartans,[75] he was probably trying to galvanize them into action with this melodramatic embellishment.

Lamachus sided with Alcibiades, and so the latter's plan was accepted. Alcibiades then went to Messana and tried to win that city over to the Athenian side. He was unable to persuade the Messanian assembly, but he apparently contacted a group of rebels there who were willing to ally with Athens.[76] The Greek world was full of this kind of intrigue, and there is reason to suspect that this plot might have worked. Laches had been successful in winning the city over during the Archidamian War,[77] and the Athenians later seemed to have had high expectations for the scheme's success.[78] Alcibiades sailed with sixty ships to Naxos and was well received there. He next went to Catana where he was at first rebuffed but later, with a little intimidation, managed to win the city over to an alliance with Athens. He did not, however, meet with any initial success at Camarina, a city that had been allied with Syracuse's enemies in the past. It is often held that Alcibiades was unsuccessful in his actualization of this plan,[79] but in a very short time he won over two strategically important cities and initiated intrigues with a third. Considering that there were only about twenty cities in Sicily of any significant size, we can easily imagine that Alcibiades' plan, given the right combination of time, intimidation, intrigue, and diplomacy, would have worked.

Time was one ingredient Alcibiades did not have. When he returned to Catana, he found that the state ship *Salaminia* had arrived there from Athens with instructions to bring him home to stand trial. Plutarch records the impeachment brought against him by Thessalus, son of Cimon.[80] Alcibiades was charged with committing sacrilege against Demeter and Kore, the goddesses of Eleusis. The officers of the *Salaminia* had been instructed not to arrest him for fear that it might cause consternation among the troops. The Athenians were also concerned that the Argives and Mantineans might desert the expedition if Alcibiades were arrested. There had been some unrest recently in Argos. The Athenians thought that the Argive friends of Alcibiades were plotting a coup against the democrats and, for this reason, they had handed some Argive hostages in their keeping over to the democrats to be executed. These events were to jeopardize the possibility that Alcibiades might stay in Argos after he escaped.

Even before Alcibiades escaped, he perpetrated his first hostile act against Athens. He somehow managed to inform the leaders of Messana about the existence of the pro-Athenian plot.[81] The conspirators were caught and executed, and the Athenians lost all chance of winning Messana over to their side. Alcibiades, along with the others who had been recalled to face charges in connection with either the herms or the Mysteries, was allowed to sail in his own ship in company with the *Salaminia*. At Thurii he and his companions abandoned their ship and escaped. The crew of the *Salaminia* were unable to locate them and soon returned to Athens.

Alcibiades was tried and condemned to death in *absentia*. His property, as well as the property of all those who had been convicted of one of the sacrileges, was confiscated and sold publicly.[82] The names of the condemned and the results of the sale of their possessions were inscribed on stelae and set up in a public place as a symbol of their disgrace.[83] The generous reward of one talent was offered to anyone who killed one of the offenders.[84] Another decree stipulated that Alcibiades' name should be cursed publicly by all the priests and priestesses.[85]

Alcibiades and his companions left Thurii in a merchant ship and sailed to Cyllene in Elis.[86] What were his options at this juncture? It is possible that Alcibiades could have gone to Persia like Themistocles before him. But Persia was soon to enter the war on the Spartan side. Her objective, the recapture of the eastern Aegean, made her the natural enemy of Athens, and this intention could have been a secret to no one. If Alcibiades had gone to Persia, it could only have been as a potential Athenian tyrant as Hippias had done a century earlier. Themistocles himself avoided a charge of treason only by death whether by natural causes or through suicide.[87] There really were no neutral states to which Alcibiades could turn. In the speech that Thucydides gives him as he addresses the Spartans, Alcibiades asserts that the man who loves his country is the one who will stop at nothing to get back there. This statement is usually dismissed as self-serving, which it certainly is, but there may be an element of truth in it. Alcibiades' vehemence is that of a lover spurned. There were other ways he might have merely saved his life, but he wanted more than that. He wanted to remain a leader, and in a sense his strategy worked; by staying in the conflict, he was eventually recalled to Athens. It is difficult to imagine that this could have happened if he had merely retired to some deserted place.

## Alcibiades in Sparta

Alcibiades accepted the invitation to come to Sparta, but he demanded of them a safe-conduct for fear of reprisals for his part in the Athenian machinations in the Peloponnese that led to the battle of Mantinea. Soon representatives from Corinth and Syracuse arrived there too to ask for assistance against the

Athenian expedition in Sicily. Alcibiades joined the Corinthians and Syracusans in asking the Spartan assembly to send aid. We have already had several opportunities to comment on the speech that Alcibiades gave to the Spartans as interpreted or imagined by Thucydides.[88] It is here that he attacked democracy and spoke of his love of Athens. Here he claimed, according to Thucydides, to have turned against the Spartans originally because they refused to deal with him at the time of the Peace of Nicias. And here too he tried to startle them with an exaggerated description of the Athenians' 'Grand Design' to become masters of the Greek world.

What mainly concerns us here is Alcibiades' practical advice to the Spartans. He advised them to send troops and an officer to Syracuse and to set up a permanent armed outpost against the Athenians at Decelea in Attica. The Spartans did not send troops to Sicily, but they did send an officer there, and they did fortify Decelea. Both of these actions had enormous repercussions and contributed to Athens' defeat not only in Sicily but also in the last decade of the Peloponnesian War.

Alcibiades' suggestions were slow to achieve fruition, and it may be that his advice was not as original or as influential as Thucydides' narrative implies.[89] The Spartans chose Gylippus to go to Syracuse. Gylippus sailed with several Corinthian ships, but experienced some difficulty and did not arrive in Syracuse until the summer. But his actions were decisive in Athens' catastrophic defeat in Sicily. The Spartans finally fortified Decelea over a year after Alcibiades reportedly advised them to do so. However, the Spartans had two strong reasons to act in the spring of 413 that they had not enjoyed in the winter of 415/414. First, they knew that the Athenian expedition was not achieving success in Sicily. Second, Athens had formally broken the peace.[90] The Spartans were responsible for initiating the Archidamian War since their allies, the Thebans, had begun the fighting and since they themselves had refused arbitration. But when the Athenians, in aiding their ally, Argos, made an attack on Laconia in the summer of 414, the Spartans were freed of all sense of responsibility in the reopening of the war.

Early in the spring of 413 the Spartans, under King Agis, invaded Attica for the first time in twelve years. They built a fort at Decelea in the mountains about fourteen miles from Athens and only slightly farther from Boeotia. If the selection of Decelea for a permanent fort was made by Alcibiades, it was well chosen. The Athenians were now deprived of their farmland all year long. The food that normally came to them from Euboea by way of Decelea now had to come by sea around Sunium. This was a further drain on Athenian finances and manpower. The Spartan fort was a magnet for escaped slaves. Over 20,000 of them, many being skilled workers, deserted Athens. Decelea remained a serious problem for the Athenians from that time until the end of the war.[91]

We can only guess at what Alcibiades' life was like during the two years he lived in Sparta. Thucydides tells us little. Plutarch tells us that Alcibiades became very popular and that he was careful to adopt Spartan customs.[92] He ate the black broth and coarse bread that was their fare, took cold baths, disciplined his body with strenuous physical exercise, and left his hair untrimmed in the Spartan manner. Plutarch speaks of Alcibiades' ability to adapt to the style of living of each country in which he found himself. In Sparta he took on Spartan manners. In Ionia with Tissaphernes he easily adopted the luxurious style of the Persians. This quality seems very characteristic of the man Alcibiades as we have come to know him.

Another aspect of Alcibiades' life in Sparta is a matter of considerable controversy. Plutarch tells us that Alcibiades seduced Timaea, the wife of King Agis, and that she became pregnant with his child.[93] When the boy was born, Timaea called him Leotychides in public, but Alcibiades in private. It is certain that, on the death of Agis, the succession was disputed.[94] Agis' brother, Agesilaus, was able to convince the authorities that Leotychides was illegitimate and hence unfit to become a king of Sparta. If we knew the exact age of Leotychides at the time he was refused the kingship, then we could have more certainty on this point. However, this information is lacking.[95] Historians are divided on the authenticity of this incident.[96]

It is certain that Alcibiades and Agis became enemies and probable that the Spartans later tried to have the former killed.[97] Westlake tried to explain the reason for the quarrel between Agis and Alcibiades and also to answer the question of what Alcibiades did during those two years by a theory he called the 'Northern Plan'.[98] According to this theory, Alcibiades went with Agis to Decelea and convinced him of the possibility of winning new support for Sparta in Thessaly, Macedonia and Chalcidice. Westlake believes that the collapse of this enterprise caused the breach between Agis and Alcibiades. There is no real evidence for a 'Northern Plan'. Hatzfeld[99] answered Westlake effectively with the contention that if Alcibiades had accompanied an enemy army into Athenian territory, this damaging fact would have found its way into the anti-Alcibiades literature.[100] There are many reasons why Alcibiades and Agis might have become enemies, but the only motives given to us by our ancient sources are the king's jealousy over the seduction of his wife and his jealousy over Alcibiades' popularity.[101]

Alcibiades seems to have aroused the jealousy and enmity of other Spartans as well.[102] By the summer of 413, he must have come to realize that he could not safely stay in Sparta much longer. No doubt he had grown tired of Spartan life also. As these tendencies coincided with the final Athenian disaster in Sicily, Alcibiades looked to Ionia both as an escape from his predicament and as a new theatre for his talents.

Chapter five

# Recall, triumph, and death

## The revolt of Athens' allies

In the wake of Athens' humiliating defeat in Sicily, her allies in
the Aegean began to revolt.[1] These states, like all the rest of
Greece, thought that Athens had been mortally wounded and
would fall to Sparta within a year. In the winter of 413/412
representatives of Euboea and Lesbos came to Agis at Decelea
with requests for aid in their revolt. Other representatives from
Chios and the Hellespont came to Sparta with similar requests in
their own rebellions from Athens. The Chians were supported by
Tissaphernes, the Persian satrap at Sardis. Pharnabazus, the
satrap of the Hellespontine district, naturally supported the
requests of the Greeks from that region. Both satraps wished to
regain Greek cities for Persia, and they were, to some extent,
rivals of each other.

Alcibiades supported the efforts of the Chians and Tissaphernes.
He used his influence with his family friend, Endius, one of the
ephors at that time, and together they persuaded the Spartans to
aid the Chians first, then the Lesbians, and after that to send
support to the Hellespont. The Spartans, in the summer of 412,
after several delays, finally sent a fleet of ships to Chios, but the
Athenians learned of their intentions, met them in a naval
engagement, and defeated them. The Spartans were discouraged
and disinclined to send out another expedition.

Alcibiades again used his influence with Endius and, according
to Thucydides,[2] stimulated his friend's rivalry with Agis. If,
Alcibiades suggested, Endius helped him to get to Chios, then
Endius and not Agis could claim credit for the revolt of Ionia and
for the Spartan alliance with Persia that was likely to ensue.
Together they persuaded the other ephors to send out Alcibiades,
the general Chalcideus, and five ships. Since the Chians would
not yet know of the Spartan naval defeat, Alcibiades was

prepared to convince them that more ships were on the way. Those Chians who were working for a revolt were still a small group of oligarchs. The majority of the island's inhabitants, according to Thucydides,[3] were unaware of the plot. The leading conspirators arranged it so that Alcibiades and Chalcideus could be introduced into a council meeting with no prior warning. Alcibiades and Chalcideus assured the Chians that more ships were coming and convinced them to revolt. Alcibiades also persuaded the mainland cities of Erythrae and Clazomenae to revolt from Athens. He then sailed to Miletus, where he had intimate contacts, and brought the people of that city into the revolt.

At about this time the Spartans, under the leadership of Chalcideus, made an arrangement with Tissaphernes. They promised to relinquish virtually all of eastern Hellas to Darius, the Great King, in return for Persian aid in defeating Athens.[4] The Spartans agreed to aid the Persians in quelling any revolts against their authority, as they were soon to do in the case of the rebel Amorges at Iasus, and to co-operate in preventing the Athenians from collecting money from their Ionian allies. It is not difficult to see Alcibiades' hand in these negotiations. He was closely associated with Chalcideus, and he was in a hurry to make an important contribution before his Spartan enemies caught up with him. If the terms of the treaty were not particularly favourable to the Peloponnesians, Alcibiades could at least claim to have obtained for them the enormous advantage of Persian aid. Considering Athens' already vulnerable state after the collapse of the Sicilian expedition, this new development might seem to ensure her defeat.

Athens, however, proved to be a tougher and more resilient foe than anyone could have guessed at the time. She built more and more triremes and sent them to Samos, which became her primary base for naval operations from this time until the end of the Peloponnesian War. An indecisive battle took place over Miletus in late summer 412 in which Alcibiades fought on the side of Tissaphernes and the Milesians.[5] Phrynichus, the future oligarch, was instrumental in convincing the Athenians not to continue the attack on Miletus when he heard of the imminent arrival of Peloponnesian reinforcements under the command of the Spartan Therimenes. Alcibiades, not knowing of the Athenian decision to retreat, advised Therimenes to rush to the aid of the Milesians. It was his last act, of which we have any knowledge, in the service of Sparta. After the Athenians withdrew, Tissaphernes put a fort and a garrison in Miletus as if to claim it for Darius.[6]

Soon after this battle, perhaps in the late autumn of 412,[7] Alcibiades took refuge with Tissaphernes. It was a matter of necessity. His enemies had gained control in Sparta and had sent instructions to Astyochus, the new naval commander in Ionia, to put him to death.

Alcibiades' position was both delicate and complex. To Tissaphernes he was still a Spartan adviser. Alcibiades had to insinuate himself into Tissaphernes' confidence and into his service in order to become the satrap's adviser. It is also probable that Alcibiades was already seeking a means to exploit his relationship with Tissaphernes in order to secure his recall to Athens.

Alcibiades spent the winter of 412/411 with Tissaphernes. The two men were well-matched in their cleverness and cunning, but Alcibiades was soon successful in gaining the satrap's confidence. Thucydides says that he became Tissaphernes' 'adviser in everything.'[8] The irony of Alcibiades' swift transformation from austere Spartan to self-indulgent Persian was lost on no one. After almost three years in Spartan company, Alcibiades probably had no trouble in making this particular transition, but he had the sensitivity as well as the good manners to adopt the style and customs of each culture in which he found himself.[9] Tissaphernes returned Alcibiades' good manners and his flatteries by naming his most beautiful park after him.[10]

Alcibiades gave Tissaphernes good advice.[11] Just as he had traded good counsel to the Spartans in return for his asylum, he did the same now to the Persian satrap. By the terms of the treaty made with the Spartans, the Persians had promised to pay the Peloponnesian sailors an Attic drachma a day. Alcibiades persuaded Tissaphernes to reduce this rate by half and to pay the sailors only at irregular intervals. If the men were paid too much, Alcibiades reasoned, they would only waste their pay on wine and other indulgences that would impair their effectiveness. And if they knew that their superiors still owed them pay that they had already earned, they would be less likely to desert. In order to institute this reduction in pay without causing rebellion, Alcibiades suggested that Tissaphernes bribe the naval commanders to aid the Persians in placating the seamen.

Alcibiades, who was undoubtedly eager to return to Athens, sought to win approval from the Athenians as well as the Persians with his next advice. He suggested to Tissaphernes that it was not in the Persians' best interests to end the war quickly. There were now three strong powers in the Aegean. A triumphant Sparta might pose an even greater threat than Athens had posed in the past. Alcibiades reminded the satrap that Sparta was traditionally

71

a land power and that she might not be content to remain behind the essentially maritime boundaries that the Athenians had maintained. Tissaphernes could call in the Phoenician navy at any time, and this fleet was easily capable of destroying the weakened Athenians. Alcibiades advised Tissaphernes not to do this. Let the Spartans and the Athenians wear each other down so that whichever side survived would be a less formidable rival to the Persians. Alcibiades again hinted that Athens might be the lesser problem in the long run.

Tissaphernes followed Alcibiades' advice. He promised the Peloponnesians that the Phoenician fleet was coming but made no effort to command it to the front. He lowered the sailors' pay and saw to it that they did not receive their money at regular intervals. As a result the Peloponnesian fleet became dispirited and suffered a consequent loss of efficiency.

The Athenians followed these developments and were aware of who was behind them. Alcibiades began to communicate with some of the Athenian leaders at Samos. He suggested that he was close to Tissaphernes and might be able to bring the Persians over to the Athenian side. However, he was unhappy with the government in Athens. Alcibiades intimated that some alteration in the existing constitution would have to be made if he were to return and if the Athenians wanted him to lead them to victory. This communication, according to Thucydides,[12] was the origin of the oligarchic coup of the Four Hundred in the year 411.

### The Phrynichus episode and the coup of the Four Hundred

The events of the year 411 are both complex and controversial. By the end of the year, Alcibiades had resumed his career in the service of Athens and had regained his influence as his city's most charismatic leader. Indeed, since he had no rival of the stature of Nicias, Alcibiades was in a more powerful position than ever before. By the end of the year, Athens had begun to recover from her devastating defeat in Sicily, but during that year she suffered two revolutions and very nearly destroyed herself in civil conflict.

Alcibiades knew the fickleness of the Athenian demos. He knew that, even if he were recalled, his popularity might not outlast his first military defeat. He also knew that his personal enemy, Androcles, was an influential leader of the people. Perhaps he hoped to secure his recall by limiting the democracy. It does not seem likely that Alcibiades actually wanted to be a part of a narrow oligarchy.[13] M.F. McGregor has suggested that he had a very devious plan in mind.[14] McGregor believes that Alcibiades 'knew exactly what he was doing . . . at all stages of his career.'[15] He planned the coup of the Four Hundred, according to this theory, in the full knowledge that he himself would not be a member of the oligarchy. Alcibiades' intention from the first, McGregor says, was to set up an oligarchy so that he, as the leader of the demos, could tear it down. McGregor points out that when Pisander first went to Athens with Alcibiades' proposals, he was greeted with 'violent protests' on the part of Alcibiades' enemies, presumably 'the demagogues.'[16] Events, however, do not seem to justify such a scenario. When Alcibiades had a chance to lead the Athenian fleet against the oligarchs, he refused.[17] Alcibiades may have had another plan in mind. I agree with McGregor that Alcibiades' enemies were the demagogues and especially the demagogue Androcles, the man who may have engineered Alcibiades' recall in 415 and who may have been the chief beneficiary of Alcibiades' downfall in that he graduated to a position of greater influence and power. My thesis, like that of McGregor, 'is not one that can be proved'.[18]

Androcles was an ambitious politician and a member of the radical democratic group that had included Hyperbolus. Alcibiades had collaborated with Nicias to ostracize Hyperbolus, probably to prevent his own ostracism. Androcles then (in 416, pp. 45–9) became the chief demagogue and a bitter enemy to Alcibiades. The next year, if my theory is right, Androcles worked with his fellow demagogues, the radical democrats, and perhaps even with the oligarchs for the ousting of Alcibiades during the scandals surrounding the Mysteries and the herms. In the speech that Thucydides gives him to deliver to the Spartans, Alcibiades accuses the demagogues of driving him out of Athens.[19] Thucydides clearly believed that the demagogues in general and Androcles in particular were to blame for the banishment of Alcibiades.[20] Is it not possible then that Alcibiades believed that he first had to be free of Androcles before he could safely return to Athens?

Alcibiades would not specifically have to demand the assassination of Androcles. By encouraging a change in the constitution, he could reasonably assume that those Athenians who felt sympathy for oligarchy would have to dispose of Androcles. Androcles and others who were 'regarded as undesirable' were, in fact, secretly murdered in 411 by young men who were working for the oligarchic cause.[21] Still, Alcibiades, having stimulated this movement, must have known that he eventually would have to deal with it. He later refused to lead the Athenian fleet against the Four Hundred in Athens, winning Thucydides' praise,[22] but this was simply intelligent strategy, for it would have meant 'the immediate occupation of Ionia and the Hellespont by the enemy'.[23] My theory is that Alcibiades did not create an oligarchy in order to destroy it but simply that he manipulated the political scene in Athens to his own advantage. He had done this successfully many times in the past, and, if he brought about the death of Androcles, it was no more than what Androcles had sought to do to him.

In the winter of 412/411,[24] Alcibiades began to send messages to some of the leading Athenians at Samos.[25] He implied that, if the democracy were changed to an oligarchy, he might return to Athenian service and bring the extensive resources of Tissaphernes with him. A deputation of those men who were interested in this prospect went to visit Alcibiades on the mainland of Asia Minor. There, Alcibiades renewed his promises of Persian aid to Athens on condition that the constitution was changed. The Athenian leaders went back to Samos and organized a coalition of people who were willing to abolish the democracy and recall Alcibiades in order to gain Persian support. Pisander became one of the leaders of this group. The general Phrynichus became the most vocal opponent of the plan. He staunchly maintained that Alcibiades was not to be trusted.

How is it possible that two men as closely aligned as Phrynichus and Pisander could have such widely divergent opinions about Alcibiades? We must first remember that politics in Athens was seldom narrowly ideological. It was fluid, connected to the issue of the moment and liable to frequent change. Phrynichus and Pisander had both been aligned with the radical democrats at an earlier stage of their careers,[26] and yet both became associated with the extreme oligarchs in the government of the Four Hundred. Pisander was apparently convinced that Alcibiades could lead Athens into an oligarchy, deliver Persian aid, and win the war against Sparta. Phrynichus was apparently not convinced of any of these propositions. According to Thucydides,[27] he argued that Alcibiades only wanted to be recalled and did not care if it were by an oligarchy or by a democracy. Phrynichus argued that Alcibiades simply wanted to shake up the status quo in order to secure his return. Thucydides says that Phrynichus believed that revolution would be bad for Athens and should be guarded against. Yet as soon as Alcibiades ceased to work for the oligarchy and threw his support to the democratic leaders in Samos, Phrynichus became one of the most ardent supporters of the revolution. He also expressed doubt that the Persians would co-operate with the Athenians.[28]

What was Phrynichus' motivation?[29] His arguments seem to have had little effect, for the majority adopted the plan and seemed to have had great hopes for its success. Phrynichus may have already had reason to fear the recall of Alcibiades. Kagan speculates that Phrynichus, during his democratic period, may have worked against Alcibiades in the wake of the scandals surrounding the mutilation of the herms and the profanation of the Mysteries.[30] This is an excellent suggestion and, as Kagan notes, would 'explain the absence of any support' for Phrynichus' arguments against Alcibiades, because the other conspirators would know of his personal motives.[31] But whether or not there were pre-existing reasons, Thucydides tells us that Phrynichus now wanted to discredit Alcibiades.[32] He feared that if, as now seemed certain, Alcibiades were recalled, he would make Phrynichus suffer for having opposed him.

The story of how Phrynichus tried to destroy his enemy is one of the most obscure and baffling episodes in Thucydides. Phrynichus sent a letter to Astyochus, the Spartan admiral, and informed him that Alcibiades was scheming to bring Tissaphernes over to the Athenian side. Phrynichus was not apparently aware that Alcibiades was no longer in the service of Sparta but was, in effect, a personal adviser to the satrap. So the irony of Phrynichus' first attempt to betray Alcibiades is that it was destined to fail, based, as it was, on the wrong assumption, i.e. that Astyochus was in a position to dispose of Alcibiades if he were so inclined. Astyochus had, in fact, already received orders from Sparta to put Alcibiades to death, and he had proved unable or unwilling to do so. Instead of trying to co-operate with Phrynichus, the Spartan naval commander went to Magnesia, met with Tissaphernes and Alcibiades and revealed to them the contents of the Athenian's letter.

It now becomes necessary to ask what was Astyochus' motivation. Thucydides, on more than one occasion, suggests that Astyochus was in the pay of Tissaphernes.[33] Astyochus' innocence on this charge has been upheld by some modern historians,[34] but whether or not he was in the pay of the satrap seems rather a moot point when we consider that the entire Spartan navy was in Tissaphernes' pay. However, it is not likely that Astyochus had surrendered his Spartan allegiance and begun to work solely for Persia. He was unpopular with the Peloponnesian sailors and was under suspicion by the Spartan authorities.[35] Since he eventually went home to face whatever charges might be brought against him,[36] it is reasonable to assume that he had some hopes of being found innocent. Astyochus probably went to Magnesia to protest against the idea of Persian aid to Athens and to negotiate further, not just to divulge the contents of Phrynichus' letter.[37]

Alcibiades, however, immediately communicated the information that he had learned from Astyochus to his contacts on Samos, accusing Phrynichus of treason and suggesting that he be put to death. Phrynichus, who was now in an even worse predicament than before, attempted to extricate himself by trying once again to conspire with Astyochus. This second attempt on the part of Phrynichus to consort with the enemy is difficult to believe especially in a man who impressed Thucydides as possessing remarkable intelligence.[38] Some scholars think that this second attempt was insincere and that Phrynichus meant to lead Astyochus into an ambush,[39] but there is no evidence for this in Thucydides. Phrynichus told Astyochus that Samos was unfortified and offered him a chance to capture the entire Athenian fleet there. Perhaps he thought that Astyochus would not be able to resist such a tempting offer.[40] However, the scheme did not work, and Astyochus informed Alcibiades as he had before. Phrynichus found out that Astyochus had betrayed him again, and so he alerted the Athenians at Samos of an imminent Spartan attack and recommended that they fortify the island. Alcibiades sent another message concerning Phrynichus' duplicity, but it had little effect since Phrynichus had cast himself in the role of defender of the island. Phrynichus went on to become one of the most extreme of the Four Hundred and one of the leaders most closely associated with the policy of betraying Athens to the Spartans.[41] He was assassinated, and his body was later disinterred and removed from Attic territory.[42] His assassins were made citizens and voted public honours.[43]

What can we conclude about this episode?[44] Phrynichus was probably both a sincere oligarch[45] and a personal enemy of Alcibiades. Whatever his democratic experience may have been in the past, he seems never again to have wavered from his commitment to oligarchy. His enmity to Alcibiades probably dated from 415 and probably related to Phrynichus' participation in the movement to condemn Alcibiades of impiety, a movement that may have inlcuded both oligarchs and radical democrats in its membership (see pp. 58–62). Phrynichus may not have seen any conflict between his enmity for Alcibiades and his desire for oligarchy. In fact, he was right to say that Alcibiades did not care for oligarchy and was simply trying to get recalled. However, the other conspirators at Samos may have known that Phrynichus had personal reasons for his opinions.[46]

Phrynichus may have been equally unaware of any conflict when he first wrote to Astyochus. He may have believed that getting rid of his personal enemy would also be a benefit to Athens. However, when Alcibiades wrote to his contacts at Samos accusing him of treason and suggesting that he be put to death, Phrynichus was no longer in a position to consider the welfare of Athens. Why did the authorities not put Phrynichus to death? It may be simply that Phrynichus was in Samos and better able to talk himself out of the difficulty while Alcibiades was not there to press the matter. Or it may be that Phrynichus began his second scheme so quickly that he did not give his fellow generals a chance to act. Some historians believe that, when Phrynichus wrote to Astyochus the second time, he already knew the Spartan navarch would betray him and that Alcibiades would again relay the information to Samos.[47] They maintain that this was all part of a master scheme. This idea is not convincing[48] and has no basis in Thucydides' narrative. Phrynichus' second letter bears all the signs of a desperate act on the part of a man who has run out of options. However, his reaction to the news that Astyochus had betrayed him and that Alcibiades was sending another letter does, to some extent, justify Thucydides' praise of Phrynichus' intelligence.[49] Phrynichus managed to extricate himself from his dilemma, but his unpopularity at Samos may have contributed to his decision to join the conspirators in Athens.

If Astyochus, as has been suggested, was primarily concerned with Spartan interests, why did he not attack Samos? The Spartans, in general, did not seem eager to fight the Athenians at sea. In spite of the Athenian losses in Sicily and the Persian aid she had acquired, Sparta was still intimidated by Athenian naval skill.[50] And in spite of her losses, Athens continued to win most of the sea battles until she was surprised and outmanoeuvred at Aegospotami. Astyochus' caution, then, was justified.[51]

Astyochus would also have been justified if he had been less than wholly convinced of Phrynichus' sincerity.[52] Perhaps Astyochus acted in Sparta's best interests. In going to Magnesia and in twice revealing the contents of Phrynichus' letters, Astyochus may have performed a service for Sparta that was both economical and profound. This scenario cannot be proved, but it goes farther than any other interpretation to explain this puzzling episode. By warning Tissaphernes of Alcibiades' plans to join the Athenians, the Spartan may have caused Tissaphernes to lose faith with Alcibiades. Astyochus may have provided the information that dissuaded the satrap from giving aid to the Athenians.[53] If this scenario is correct, Astyochus helped Tissaphernes to see that Alcibiades was not his adviser any longer, but was only using him to pave his way back to Athens. This interpretation might also explain why the negotiations between Alcibiades and Tissaphernes, on the Persian side, and the Athenian oligarchs came to such an unsuccessful conclusion. It would also be an ironic footnote to this episode if Alcibiades and Phrynichus, two of the wiliest manipulators in Greek history, had been outwitted by the supposedly naïve and ineffective Spartan.[54]

Despite Phrynichus' opposition, the oligarchic party at Samos voted to send Pisander and others to Athens to negotiate for the recall of Alcibiades and the overthrow of the democracy. There was opposition in Athens where many citizens were not eager to alter the constitution. The enemies of Alcibiades and the priests of Eleusis were also loud in their denunciations of this plan.[55] Pisander, however, speaking to an assembly of the Athenian people, finally persuaded them that they could not win the war without Persian aid, and that they could not obtain this aid without limiting the democracy and recalling Alcibiades. Pisander also arranged to have Phrynichus removed from his command, on an unrelated charge, but, really, according to Thucydides,[56] because of his opposition to the negotiations with Alcibiades. Pisander also made contact with the hetaireiai and urged them to get rid of the democracy. With the approval of the Athenian assembly, Pisander and his ten associates[57] then set sail for Ionia in order to make an arrangement with Tissaphernes and Alcibiades.

These negotiations never reached a satisfactory conclusion, and the reason for this is far from clear. Alcibiades, at the court of Tissaphernes on behalf of his host, claimed Ionia and all the islands off its coast for Persia, a condition to which Pisander and his associates agreed. Alcibiades next demanded that the Great King should have the right to build ships and patrol his own coast. The Athenian diplomats refused this condition since it would threaten not only the remainder of their empire but the security of mainland Greece as well. Pisander and his associates left for Samos, angry at what they considered Alcibiades' treachery.[58] This much is clear, but what was Alcibiades' motive in this conference? Perhaps he had promised Persian support in good faith but was unable to convince Tissaphernes. Or is it possible that Alcibiades did not want to strengthen the oligarchic faction and that he deliberately sabotaged the negotiations? Thucydides gives us a somewhat confused picture. At 8.56.3 the historian hints that Alcibiades and Tissaphernes were in agreement not to come to terms with Athens, whereas at 8.52.1 Alcibiades was still trying to persuade Tissaphernes to aid the Athenians.[59] The usual explanation, that Alcibiades had simply given up trying to get Persian support for Athens and acquiesced to the will of Tissaphernes, is quite possibly right. However, it seems uncharacteristically inept of Alcibiades to invite his supporters to come to the court of Tissaphernes, knowing that he would have to send them away empty-handed. M.F. McGregor's thesis, that Alcibiades was 'unwilling rather than unable to establish a satisfactory liaison between Tissaphernes and the Athenian oligarchs',[60] is, at least, as credible as the more usual explanation that Alcibiades had been outmanoeuvred by Tissaphernes. Thucydides could not have known what was going on behind the scenes. Even if Alcibiades himself had reported to Thucydides, it is likely that the former would have given the historian a self-serving interpretation of the facts. If the scenario outlined above concerning Phrynichus and Astyochus is correct then Tissaphernes had only recently become disenchanted with Alcibiades. Perhaps Alcibiades had nothing more to gain from this encounter than the preservation of the illusion that he was still an important adviser to the satrap. If he had allowed this illusion to evaporate, then it is possible that he would not have been recalled by either oligarchs or democrats. As far as we know, this was the end of Alcibiades' flirtation with oligarchy. His contacts with Athenians from this point on would be with those of his fellow countrymen who favoured democracy. His treatment of Pisander and the other representatives may even have been his way of notifying those leaders on Samos who were not sympathetic to oligarchy that he was willing to serve their cause.[61]

Pisander returned to Samos, bitter at Alcibiades' conduct, but determined to continue the revolution none the less. He and his associates tried to arrange an oligarchic coup in Samos itself. They joined forces with a group of native Samians, who carried out certain acts of terror including the assassination of Hyperbolus, the man who had been ostracized with the co-operation of Alcibiades and Nicias in 416 (see p. 000) and who had been residing in Samos at the time. The attempted coup was not a success, and Samos remained a bastion of Athenian democracy even after Athens itself temporarily became an oligarchy.

By the time that Pisander returned to Athens, the conspiracy was well under way. Phrynichus, after he was relieved of his command, overcame his qualms about internal strife and joined the movement. Other leaders of the coup were Antiphon, the brilliant rhetorician, and Theramenes, who eventually emerged as the leader of the moderate faction. The Athenian conspirators also committed certain acts of terror including the assassination of Androcles, previously mentioned. Pisander called an assembly outside the city at Colonus. The assembly voted to end the payment of salaries to magistrates and to relieve the incumbent magistrates from the remainder of their terms of office. The conspirators also created a council of Four Hundred. The Four Hundred were supposed eventually to convene a larger body of Five Thousand, but they never did this. A few days later the conspirators drove the boule out of its chamber and took over the government. The Four Hundred remained in office for over three months and became, in effect, the oligarchic government of Athens. They silenced their enemies with murder, imprisonment, and exile and, in general, instituted a regime of brutal intimidation and repression.[62]

## The recall of Alcibiades

News of these events in Athens reached the navy on Samos. The generals Thrasybulus and Thrasyllus persuaded the forces there that the Athenians at Samos must maintain the democratic tradition even if the mother-city had become temporarily an oligarchy. The men swore oaths to uphold the democratic constitution of Athens, to continue the war against Sparta, and to view the Four Hundred as their enemies.[63] The democratic leaders, and especially Thrasybulus, pressed those assembled to recall Alcibiades. Their view prevailed and so it was that Alcibiades was recalled, not by Athens proper, but by the democratic government-in-exile at Samos.

Alcibiades spoke to an assembly of the soldiers at Samos. He exaggerated his influence with Tissaphernes. He did this, according to Thucydides, for three reasons: to bolster his own reputation among them, to frighten the Four Hundred, and to discourage the Peloponnesians by casting doubt on their relationship with the Persian satrap.[64] Alcibiades said that Tissaphernes would bring up the Phoenician fleet to aid the Athenians instead of the Peloponnesians if he (Alcibiades) were allowed to lead them. He said, according to Thucydides, that the satrap was prepared to sell his own bed, if that were necessary, and would go to any lengths to support the Athenians as long as he could trust them. Alcibiades had already been recalled, but this speech apparently roused the soldiers to great enthusiasm. They elected him general and looked to him as their chief strategist. The men were so encouraged that they wanted to sail to Athens immediately and pull down the government of the Four Hundred. Alcibiades had to talk them out of that self-destructive idea.[65]

Shortly after that assembly, delegates from the Four Hundred came to Samos. Another assembly[66] was held in which the delegates spoke to the army in an attempt to mollify them. The attempt was unsuccessful, and the soldiers became so angry that they again proposed sailing out to the Piraeus and waging war against the Four Hundred. Alcibiades again talked them out of it, and Thucydides thought that no other man then alive would have been able to persuade them at that time.[67] Plutarch saw accurately that in this deed Alcibiades performed a great service for Athens.

> On this occasion, at least, there is no doubt that he saved the Athenian empire. If the fleet had sailed home, the whole of Ionia, the Hellespont and the islands might have fallen into the enemy's hands without a blow being struck, while Athenian would have fought Athenian and carried the war inside their own city walls. The fact that none of this came to pass was thanks to Alcibiades more than to any other man.[68]

Alcibiades, speaking for the army, said that he would negotiate with the Five Thousand but implied that he would not come to terms with the Four Hundred. He advised the delegates to get rid of the Four Hundred, reinstate the Council of Five Hundred, and to make no concessions to the Spartans. He would support any efforts they could make toward economy, and he assured them that, if these measures were adopted, Athens and the army at Samos could join forces and defeat the Peloponnesians. This advice, when the delegates returned home and reported it, helped to widen the schism that already existed within the Four Hundred. Antiphon and Phrynichus, who represented the extremists, led a party to Sparta in hopes of making peace on almost any terms they could get. They also began to build a wall in the port at Eetioneia. They said that the purpose of the wall was to protect Athens from the army at Samos. Theramenes began to move away from the leaders of the Four Hundred and to call for the appointment of the Five Thousand. He maintained that the purpose of the wall at Eetioneia was not to keep the army out but to let the Peloponnesians in. Theramenes' moderate faction eventually won the struggle, and they handed the government of Athens over to the Five Thousand.[69] This new government soon recalled Alcibiades[70] and sent a message to Samos ordering the forces there to prosecute the war with vigour.

## The Hellespontine War

The war in the Aegean now entered a new phase. The Spartan admiral Astyochus, possibly under the influence of Tissaphernes, had been inactive. The Spartans replaced Astyochus with Mindarus, and Mindarus abandoned the association with Tissaphernes for the more promising offer of Pharnabazus, the satrap of the Hellespontine region. Pharnabazus promised to provide the pay that Tissaphernes, on Alcibiades' recommendation, had been supplying only intermittently and insufficiently. Consequently, Mindarus led the Spartan navy north to begin new operations in the Hellespont. He was pursued by Thrasybulus and Thrasyllus, who met him in battle and defeated him at Cynossema in late August or early September 411.

Earlier, perhaps by two weeks, Alcibiades had sailed in the direction of Aspendus in the south where Tissaphernes had gone ostensibly to call up the Phoenician fleet to help the Spartans. Alcibiades probably had no realistic hope of bringing the Phoenician fleet to the aid of the Athenians, but he hoped to create suspicion in the minds of the Spartans by intimating that he and Tissaphernes were still allies.[71] To this extent his mission was a success, because the Spartans never again trusted Tissaphernes. Alcibiades then sailed back to Samos and took credit for Tissaphernes' decision not to send the Phoenician fleet to the aid of the Spartans.[72] He then went to Halicarnassus, where he gathered money, and to Cos, which he fortified. When Alcibiades returned to Samos, he probably received information concerning the recent operations in the Hellespont. So he sailed there and arrived in time to relieve the Athenians, who had been fighting a long and indecisive battle off Abydus.[73]

The Spartan ally, Dorieus of Thurii, had been attempting to bring reinforcements to Mindarus at Abydus. The Athenians at Sestus, under the leadership of Thrasybulus and Thrasyllus, learned of Dorieus' coming and attacked him. Mindarus, in turn, attacked the Athenians with his entire fleet. The battle continued from early morning until late in the day without either side able to win a clear victory. When Alcibiades arrived with eighteen ships, each side hoped that the reinforcements had come for them. Alcibiades raised a purple flag from his ship, which was a prearranged signal to the Athenians that he was bringing help.

The Peloponnesian ships fled to the mainland where they were supported by Pharnabazus and his infantry. The Athenians pursued them to the shore, fought them and captured thirty of their ships. Alcibiades' participation in this battle was decisive, and the Athenians could begin to look toward the future with greater optimism.

Tissaphernes came north to the Hellespont apparently in an attempt to regain the trust of the Peloponnesians. Alcibiades went to see Tissaphernes, soon after the battle of Abydus, perhaps in November 411. He was arrested and sent to Sardis as a prisoner. What did Alcibiades now hope to gain from Tissaphernes? Perhaps he thought that he still had to preserve the illusion that he was a close friend of the satrap's in order to maintain his prestige among the Athenians.[74] Thucydides says that Alcibiades had followed Tissaphernes to Aspendus only to embarrass him in the eyes of the Peloponnesians.[75] If they thought that Tissaphernes was still the friend of Alcibiades, now clearly in Athenian service, they could only conclude that it was not in their best interest to continue their association with the satrap. But the Peloponnesians were now clearly working with Pharnabazus, and Tissaphernes was vainly trying to woo them back. It would have been an inopportune and seemingly unnecessary venture for Alcibiades to embarrass Tissaphernes further. Alcibiades might have genuinely believed that the satrap would deliver aid to the Athenians, and Tissaphernes may have encouraged him in this belief in order to lure him into captivity. The satrap perhaps thought that arresting Alcibiades might repair his tattered relationship with the Spartans. Xenophon says only that Tissaphernes had orders from the Great King to make war on the Athenians.[76]

After thirty days in prison, Alcibiades managed to escape on a horse from Sardis to Clazomenae.[77] He escaped in the company of a man named Mantitheus, presumably the same man he left in charge of the Hellespont (along with another man named Diodorus) when he went home to Athens in 407.[78] In one last effort to revenge himself on Tissaphernes, Alcibiades spread the rumour that the satrap had freed him on purpose.[79] There was little need for Alcibiades to persist in discrediting Tissaphernes for the Spartans; it is clear that they no longer intended to collaborate with him. Moreover, Alcibiades' relationship with the satrap was also at an end. He could no longer hope for Persian support for Athens, or even to use the possibility of Persian support as a weapon in his diplomatic arsenal.

Meanwhile, the Athenian generals at Sestus had learned that the Peloponnesians were gathering a large force across the

Hellespont at Abydus, and they were afraid that Mindarus was planning to attack them. The Athenian forces were significantly reduced at this time since Thrasybulus was at Thasos and Theramenes was in Macedonia. Both generals were engaged in collecting money. The generals at Sestus decided to retreat to Cardia on the other side of the Thracian Chersonese. Alcibiades managed to obtain several triremes and sailed from Clazomenae to Cardia. The Athenians learned that Mindarus had led the Peloponnesian fleet away from Abydus and was apparently on his way to Cyzicus. Alcibiades crossed the Chersonese on land to Sestus and commanded the Athenian fleet to sail around and meet him there. At Sestus Alcibiades was also joined by Thrasybulus and Theramenes and their ships.[80] The Athenians learned that Mindarus, with the help of Pharnabazus, had captured Cyzicus.

The events surrounding the battle of Cyzicus are narrated differently by our two major sources. Neither the account of Xenophon nor that of Diodorus is wholly satisfactory, and elements of both[81] have been incorporated into this biography. Diodorus' narrative, however, is more circumstantial and is probably the better source, on the whole, for this particular episode.[82]

The Athenians sailed past the enemy camp at Abydus by night so that the Spartans would not know the size of their fleet.[83] They proceeded to the island of Proconnesus where they spent the night. The next day Alcibiades addressed the troops. He told them to be prepared to fight on land and sea. He admonished them, according to Xenophon,[84] to fight all the harder since the Pelponnesians had all the resources of the Great King of Persia, and the Athenians had to rely on their wits alone. They then set out to meet the enemy. The Athenians disembarked a land force on the mainland, under the command of Chaereas, with instructions to march against Cyzicus. Alcibiades, Theramenes, and Thrasybulus then divided the ships among themselves. Alcibiades took his squadron on ahead in order to draw the enemy out to fight. Mindarus saw Alcibiades' ships, perhaps forty in number,[85] and set sail to engage in battle. Alcibiades retreated until he had drawn Mindarus out for a sufficient distance from the shore, and then he turned around and advanced. The squadrons of Thrasybulus and Theramenes, who had been hiding behind a promontory,[86] sailed out into the open. Alcibiades' plan probably envisioned the total encirclement of Mindarus by Theramenes and Thrasybulus. Theramenes apparently took the eastern path toward the mainland, and Thrasybulus the western route.[87] If the two generals had successfully completed the encirclement, then the Athenians could have destroyed the Peloponnesian fleet at sea. This part of the scheme must not have gone entirely as planned, but it was successful to the extent that it prevented Mindarus from returning to port. He was forced to land at a place that the ancient sources call Cleri, but he was fortunate enough to join with a portion of Pharnabazus' army. Alcibiades followed him and destroyed or rendered inoperative most of the Peloponnesian ships. The two sides then engaged in an intense land battle.

Thrasybulus sent Theramenes after the infantry under Chaereas. He then landed his own men on the shore, apparently to the east of Cleri,[88] with the intention of coming to the aid of Alcibiades. Mindarus sent the Spartan commander Clearchus with some Peloponnesians and Persian mercenaries to fight the new arrivals. Thrasybulus' men fought hard, but were beginning to lose ground when Theramenes arrived with his own men as well as the foot soldiers under Chaereas. These reinforcements proved too strong for the enemy who began to retreat, first the Persian mercenaries and then the Peloponnesians.

Meanwhile Alcibiades was still fighting Mindarus' troops near the ships. When the forces of Theramenes arrived to aid Alcibiades, Mindarus sent half his men to meet them. Mindarus took an active part in the hostilities, fighting heroically, according to Diodorus,[89] but he was eventually killed by Alcibiades' men. Once Mindarus was dead, the Peloponnesians and their allies fled. Pharnabazus and the Peloponnesians abandoned Cyzicus, and so the Athenians regained the city without further bloodshed.

There can be no doubt that Alcibiades was the leading force behind the victory. Xenophon and Plutarch both stress his leadership, but it is Diodorus' version that shows Alcibiades' mind at work. Alcibiades would not set sail in the middle of a storm, as Xenophon's account would have it, with no idea of how he would challenge the enemy.[90] He had a plan, and this plan involved his usual combination of shrewdness and daring. Alcibiades deceived Mindarus into attacking what he thought was an inferior force. Mindarus was unprepared for battle, and, when he was forced to land, he had to fight the Athenians on several fronts. Alcibiades had risked most of Athens' resources and his own military future on a dangerous and ambitious venture, but the rewards of the victory were great.

The Athenians had effectively destroyed the Spartan navy. Shortly afterward they intercepted a letter to Sparta from Hippocrates, Mindarus' vice-admiral, that read: 'The ships are lost. Mindarus is dead. The men are hungry. We do not know what to do.'[91] The Athenians were soon admitted to Perinthus and received money from Selymbria. They established a fort at Chrysopolis which again gave them control of the Black Sea and re-established the flow of grain from that region to Athens.

## The battles of Chalcedon and Byzantium

According to Diodorus,[92] the Spartans sent ambassadors to Athens with a proposal of peace shortly after the battle of Cyzicus. The embassy was led by Endius, Alcibiades' family friend. Endius proposed that each side keep the cities currently in its possession and that they exchange prisoners on the basis of one Spartan for one Athenian. He also suggested that the Spartans would give up their garrison at Decelea if the Athenians would give up theirs at Pylos. The Athenians, under the influence of Cleophon, rejected the offer. Cleophon was a radical leader in the tradition of Cleon, Hyperbolus, and Androcles. He was probably not a political ally of Alcibiades, but on this issue the two men were doubtless in agreement. Diodorus condemns the Athenians for rejecting the peace,[93] and, indeed, it appears in retrospect to have been a poor decision. But given the conditions that existed immediately after the battle of Cyzicus, Endius' offer could not have seemed desirable. The Peloponnesian navy had been destroyed. Athens was in an advantageous position to regain quickly much of her lost territory, which still included Euboea, Rhodes, Thasos, Chios, Selymbria, Chalcedon, and Byzantium as well as a large portion of the west coast of Asia Minor.[94] Athens' prospects had improved so greatly within the past year that to submit to Endius' proposals was tantamount to surrender.

Alcibiades' primary concern in the next two years (410–408) was the securing of the Bosporus.[95] The Spartans sent Clearchus with fifteen ships to aid Byzantium and Chalcedon against Athens, probably during the winter of 410/409.[96] Although three of the ships were sunk by the Athenians, the remainder arrived safely at Byzantium. Alcibiades was not ready to attack these two strategically important cities. For the moment the Athenians had to rely on their fort at Chrysopolis to keep the Bosporus open. Alcibiades does not seem to have taken part in a major battle throughout the year of 409.[97] Most of the campaigns of that year were modest in scope and of only minor significance. The Spartans recovered Pylos, which had been in enemy hands since 425.[98] The Athenians sent out Thrasyllus with fifty triremes to help win back Athenian allies in Ionia. Thrasyllus was victorious at Colophon, but he failed to regain Ephesus. After this setback, he joined Alcibiades at Sestus.[99]

At first Alcibiades' men were reluctant to fraternize with Thrasyllus' men since the latter had just been defeated, and the men under Alcibiades claimed never to have known defeat.[100] This incident shows that, in spite of the hardships and the limited resources of the Athenians, Alcibiades' men were imbued with a sense of optimism concerning the outcome of the war.[101] Alcibiades tried to unify the men under his command with those under Thrasyllus in the winter of 409/408 while fortifying the city of Lampsacus on the southern coast of the Hellespont. However, it was not until they campaigned against Abydus that Thrasyllus' men and Alcibiades' original group began to co-operate fully. Pharnabazus led his cavalry to the defence of Abydus, but he was defeated. The satrap fled, and Alcibiades pursued him until nightfall.[102]

In spring 408 the Athenians proceeded against Chalcedon. The Chalcedonians, who learned that the Athenians were going to attack their city, entrusted their portable property to their neighbours, the Bithynians. Alcibiades went to the Bithynians and demanded the Chalcedonian property. He threatened to declare war on them as well if they did not comply. The Bithynians delivered the property and agreed to a treaty with the Athenians.[103]

The Athenians built an encircling wall around Chalcedon in order to blockade it. Xenophon says that it extended from sea to sea,[104] meaning from the Sea of Marmara (Propontis) to the Bosporus. The wall also had to be built to the bank of a river and continued on the other side, so it was a difficult undertaking. The Spartan harmost was a man named Hippocrates, possibly the same man who sent the laconic message of desperation to Sparta after the battle of Cyzicus that was intercepted by the Athenians.[105] Hippocrates led his troops into battle against the Athenians. Outside the wall, Pharnabazus attacked the Athenians with both foot soldiers and cavalry, but he was unable to breach the Athenian wall and so was of little use to the Chalcedonians. Thrasyllus fought Hippocrates for a long time until Alcibiades brought reinforcements.[106] Hippocrates was slain, and his men retreated back into the city.

Soon after this battle in summer 408 Alcibiades sailed to the Hellespont to raise money. He left Thrasyllus and the other generals to come to terms with Pharnabazus. Pharnabazus gave the Athenians twenty talents and agreed to lead Athenian ambassadors to the Great King of Persia. Alcibiades gathered money and reinforcements from the Chersonese and other parts of Thrace. His destination was Byzantium, but he delayed long enough to recapture Selymbria, which had revolted by 410. After the battle of Cyzicus the Selymbrians had paid the Athenians money but refused them entrance into their city. Alcibiades arranged to have Selymbria betrayed by agents within.[107] Portions of the treaty that he made with the conquered city, which was eventually ratified by Athens a year later, are extant.[108]

Alcibiades next turned his attention to Byzantium. His plan for the capture of this city was much the same as the one he had used against Chalcedon. He began by building a blockading wall around the city. The Spartan harmost was Clearchus, and he had with him detachments of Megarians under Helixus and Boeotians under Coeratadas. Clearchus made himself unpopular with the Byzantines by reserving the food supplies for his garrison and allowing the city's population to go hungry. Perhaps for this reason, Alcibiades was able to persuade some of the Byzantines to betray their city. The siege promised to be a stalemate until Clearchus, leaving the city under the command of Helixus and Coeratadas, sailed away in order to get help from Pharnabazus. Alcibiades' agents within Byzantium chose this opportunity to open the city to the Athenians.[109] They opened the gates at night, and the Athenians took possession of the city before anyone inside was aware of their actions. Helixus and Coeratadas surrendered when they discovered that it was too late and that the Athenians were in control. The two leaders were sent to Athens for imprisonment, but Coeratadas escaped and made his way to Agis at Decelea.

### Alcibiades' return to Athens

The victories at Chalcedon and Byzantium strengthened Athenian control of the Bosporus and assured the continued flow of grain from the Black Sea region to Attica. Alcibiades had enjoyed enormous success since he joined the fleet in 411. Athens had been on the brink of collapse at that time, but Alcibiades' string of brilliant victories had made an important contribution toward the restoration of her empire and, with it, the restoration of her confidence as well. Alcibiades now decided that it was time to go home to Athens. He sailed south first to the region of Caria and collected a hundred talents, and then he sailed back to Samos. Thrasyllus sailed to Athens with the main fleet. Alcibiades took twenty ships and sailed to Paros and from there to Gytheium, where he observed the Spartans building new triremes. Alcibiades apparently delayed his return long enough to hear that he and his friends had been elected to the board of generals for the year. Still insecure about his reception, he approached Attica modestly as the leader of a small squadron, not as the commander of the fleet.[110] Xenophon says that when Alcibiades sailed into the Piraeus he was filled with apprehension.[111] The superstitious noted that he returned to Athens during the rite of the Plynteria, the holiday on which the robes of Athena Polias were purified. The priests veiled the statue during the purification, and so it seemed to the credulous that Athena was hiding from Alcibiades and rejecting him.[112]

Standing on the deck of his ship, Alcibiades saw Euryptolemus, his cousin, and then he began to recognize friends and other members of his family. He went to the city surrounded by people who wished to protect him and others who merely wished to see him. Protection was unnecessary for Alcibiades had reached the apex of his popularity. He still had enemies, but on that day they were silent. Alcibiades spoke before both the boule and the assembly. If Thucydides had lived to compose this section of his *History*, he probably would have given us a memorable speech, for Alcibiades never had a better opportunity to exercise his oratorical skills. Xenophon says only that Alcibiades pleaded his innocence on the charge of sacrilege and maintained that he had been unjustly treated.[113]

There can be little doubt that Alcibiades' speech was a success. The people voted that his property, which had been confiscated and sold, be returned to him.[114] They agreed to throw into the sea the stelae on which had been recorded all the charges against him.[115] They voted that the priests who had cursed him by decree of the people revoke their curses.[116] And, most importantly, they voted him supreme commander.[117] Alcibiades had, if only for a few months, acquired the mantle of Pericles, the goal for which he had laboured all his life.

Alcibiades chose to lead a procession of the Athenian people to Eleusis as an appropriate symbol of reconciliation.[118] If Alcibiades had been guilty of profaning the Mysteries, there is reason to believe that he was repentant. He had certainly paid a heavy price for his foolishness. At any rate the symbolism of the act was irresistible. Ever since Agis and his soldiers had fortified Decelea, the Athenians had been forced to make their ceremonial journey by sea to Eleusis for the Mysteries. As a result they had to omit many aspects of the ritual. Alcibiades made his plans known to the Eumolpidae and the Kerykes. He led the procession himself and protected it the entire way with his infantry. If Agis had attacked, Alcibiades could have led the Athenians in a holy cause. Agis did not attack and thereby made his garrison look cowardly and ineffective. The episode was a personal triumph for Alcibiades. It was to be his final triumph.

## Alcibiades' second fall

While Alcibiades was in Athens, other events of great importance were taking place. Darius II (424–405) sent his son Cyrus to take charge of Persian interests in western Asia Minor. Both Darius and Cyrus wished to aid the Spartans without reservation, and neither intended to tolerate either the duplicity of Tissaphernes or the ineffectiveness of Pharnabazus. At the same time the Spartans discovered in Lysander their most effective leader since Brasidas. Lysander sailed east and met with Cyrus at Sardis in 407, and the two men formed a close and co-operative relationship, one that would prove disastrous to Athens. Lysander persuaded Cyrus to raise the sailors' pay to four obols a day.[119] This increase was a blow to the Athenians who were having difficulty finding three obols for their own men. Some sailors deserted to the Spartans, and those that remained suffered a loss of morale. Raising money became as important an activity for the Athenian leaders as winning battles.

When Alcibiades left Athens in autumn 407, he sailed to Gaurium on the island of Andros.[120] Andros had revolted from the Athenian Empire and was now under the domination of a Spartan garrison. The Athenians defeated the army of Andrians and Peloponnesians and besieged the city. Alcibiades did not wait to see the end of the siege but sailed on to Samos for the further prosecution of the war. It was probably here that Alcibiades first learned of the new arrangements between Cyrus and Lysander. Perhaps it was his idea to send ambassadors to Cyrus through Tissaphernes.[121] Tissaphernes urged Cyrus to follow his policy, the one that Alcibiades had recommended, and to allow the Athenians and the Spartans to wear each other out. Cyrus was not moved by the arguments of Tissaphernes and sent the Athenian ambassadors away.

Meanwhile, Lysander was having the Spartan fleet repaired at Ephesus. When Alcibiades learned of this he sailed to the harbour with the intention of engaging Lysander in a naval battle. Lysander did not accept the challenge, and Alcibiades, in spring 406, made his temporary headquarters at Notium on the northern side of the bay near Ephesus. Alcibiades, leaving the fleet under the command of his pilot Antiochus with orders not to engage Lysander in battle, went north, probably to join Thrasybulus at Phocaea.[122]

There is disagreement in the sources about where Alcibiades went. Xenophon says that he went to Phocaea.[123] Plutarch follows this version in the *Lysander*[124], but in the *Alcibiades* he says that Alcibiades went to Caria to collect money.[125] Nepos records Cyme as the place of Alcibiades' downfall.[126] Diodorus says that he went to Clazomenae and that later, after he had returned to Notium, he went on a hostile campaign against the Athenian ally of Cyme.[127] We cannot be certain that this raid is historical, but if it is, it would help explain some of the confusion in the sources. The following is a speculative scenario. Alcibiades left the fleet at Notium and went to aid Thrasybulus at Phocaea. As soon as he heard of Antiochus' defeat, he returned to Notium and attempted to engage Lysander in battle. Failing that, Alcibiades realized that without a definitive victory in some arena, his career with Athens was finished. Victories required money, and Alcibiades had none. In this desperate frame of mind, he resolved to stage a raid immediately in order to raise money for an assault, perhaps on Ephesus. Cyme came to his mind because he had just been in neighbouring Phocaea. When the Cyme campaign failed, Alcibiades was resigned to banishment. This scenario would explain why Nepos thought that Alcibiades met his downfall at Cyme and why Plutarch thought that he left Notium to go away and collect money. Plutarch may have misremembered Alcibiades' destination, or it is possible that Cyme became Caria through scribal error. It is still not clear, if this incident actually happened, whether the Athenians were angry at Alcibiades because he attacked an ally (Diodorus) or because he failed in the attempt (Nepos).

The Athenians were also angry at Alcibiades for leaving his pilot Antiochus in charge of the fleet. In whose hands should he have left the fleet? There were probably no other generals at Notium since Conon seems to have been left in charge of the siege at Andros, and Aristocrates and Adeimantus most probably accompanied Alcibiades to Phocaea.[128] Under these circumstances, we would expect that an admiral would ordinarily choose a trierarch to leave in charge. If this was the customary procedure, as apparently it was, Alcibiades paid dearly for his refusal to follow it. But we must emphasize, as does Kagan,[129] that Alcibiades did not expect his designated lieutenant to initiate or accept any military engagements. The trierarchs were ship commanders whose primary qualification was that they were rich enough to pay for the maintenance of the ship. Alcibiades had known Antiochus for almost twenty years (see p. 31), and he probably believed that the pilot knew more about naval procedures and warfare than any of the trierarchs, who were essentially amateurs. It is also possible that Alcibiades wanted to avoid jealousy among the trierarchs or that he had some private plans that he believed Antiochus alone capable of handling.

The battle of Notium presents a number of problems with the sources and a few problems not answered by any of the sources.[130] As so often in this period, we must choose between two alternative traditions represented by Xenophon and Diodorus. Diodorus, as was stated in the Preface, follows Ephorus in the period. Ephorus, in turn, was probably influenced by the author of the *Hellenica Oxyrhynchia*. We have a fragment of the latter concerning the battle of Notium. In the *Hellenica Oxyrhynchia* fragment, someone (obviously Antiochus) took ten triremes and sailed in the direction of Ephesus, apparently trying to lure some enemy ships out to battle. Lysander sent out a few ships at first, but then he continued to send out vessels until he had launched his entire fleet. Antiochus' trireme was captured and sunk. The main Athenian fleet came to the rescue of the remainder of Antiochus' squadron, but they were defeated and lost twenty-two ships. Diodorus' account conforms in most essentials to that of the Oxyrhynchus historian. Xenophon's account differs in certain details. Here, Antiochus sailed to Ephesus with his own and only one other ship, and the Athenians lost only fifteen triremes.

The major difficulty in all the descriptions of the battle of Notium is the unanswered question of what it was that Antiochus hoped to achieve. Was he trying to lure out the Peloponnesians to a trap, to repeat, that is, the strategy of the battle of Cyzicus?[131] It does not seem possible that he hoped to attract the entire Spartan fleet with two triremes. Either Antiochus hoped to lure out a few ships with his two and surprise them with another eight that were hidden, or he hoped to lure out all or most of the Peloponnesians and surprise them with the entire Athenian fleet. Since both Diodorus and Xenophon stress that the Athenians were unprepared and undisciplined, the latter alternative seems unlikely. The *Hellenica Oxyrhynchia* tells us that Lysander at first sent out only three ships,[132] a fact not found in the other sources.

The most likely scenario then is that Antiochus, as a minor exercise, attempted to capture a few enemy ships using, in miniature, the strategy of the battle of Cyzicus. He left Notium with ten ships, hid eight of them and sailed toward Ephesus with only two. Lysander launched a few ships, perhaps the three mentioned in the *Hellenica Oxyrhynchia*. The Peloponnesians sank Antiochus' trireme, drowning the pilot. Lysander continued to send out more vessels that chased the other Athenian ship away. The hidden eight triremes also retreated. The Athenians at Notium saw their own ships being chased by the Peloponnesians and came to their rescue. But, since they were unprepared and had no leader, they were undisciplined and lost the battle.[133] The Athenians may have lost either fifteen triremes, as Xenophon says, or twenty-two, in Diodorus' version,[134] but most of their crews escaped. It was only a minor victory for the Peloponnesians, but it was a major embarrassment for Alcibiades. As soon as he heard about the defeat, he returned to the fleet and attempted to challenge Lysander to another battle, but Lysander no longer had anything to gain from a confrontation with Alcibiades.

Alcibiades' enemies now mounted a campaign against him. A Thrasybulus (not the general) and other soldiers from Samos sailed to Athens in order to add their voices to those already there denouncing him.[135] There may have been other charges against him.[136] The soldiers from Samos accused him of secret negotiations with Pharnabazus and of favouring the enemy.[137] There were also the usual charges of private immorality.[138] But dereliction of duty in connection with the battle of Notium was probably the primary charge.[139] Many Athenians apparently believed that Alcibiades should have stayed with the fleet, or, if he could not, should not have left it in the hands of his pilot, an unusual and seemingly capricious procedure. The Athenians chose new generals, and Alcibiades was not among them. Conon sailed from Andros to Samos where he relieved him of his command.[140] If this seems unfair treatment of Alcibiades, we should only consider the fate of those generals who replaced him. Eight of them were in command of the Athenian victory at Arginusae only a few months after Notium. In spite of their victory, six generals were tried and executed for failing to rescue drowning men from some of their own wrecked ships.[141]

## Alcibiades' final days

In the summer of 406 Alcibiades retreated to one of the castles that he owned in the Thracian Chersonese. He may have had as many as three different castles in the Hellespontine region,[142] at least one of which was at Pactye, about twenty miles from

Aegospotami, where Athens would soon meet a devastating defeat. After Conon relieved him of his command, Alcibiades took one trireme and withdrew to Pactye.[143] He seems to have supplemented this crew with some mercenaries and to have created a small private army.[144] He apparently became something of a robber baron at the expense of the native Thracian tribes, and he negotiated on terms of equality with several Thracian kings.[145] This period of Alcibiades' life is unusually obscure, but there can be little doubt that he survived and apparently prospered for a year as a pirate in Thrace.

Alcibiades may still have cherished hopes of returning to Athens. There were undoubtedly still those, especially after the trial of the generals, who saw him as the city's most capable leader.[146] Precisely for this reason, other Athenians saw Alcibiades as the major threat to their own ambitions.

The final battle of the war was fought at Aegospotami.[147] After Lysander captured the city of Lampsacus, the Athenians followed him to the Hellespont. They anchored their fleet on the other side of the strait at Aegospotami. For several days they attempted to engage Lysander in battle, but the Spartans would not sail out and fight them. Alcibiades observed the Athenians, who were camped near his castle at Pactye, and approached them with a proposition. If they would offer him a share in the command, he would furnish them aid, not only his own band of followers but also soldiers under the command of the Thracian kings Medocus and Seuthes. The Athenian generals turned down his offer, perhaps thinking (as was undoubtedly the case) that if they won, Alcibiades would get all the credit, but if they lost, the blame would be theirs alone. Before he left the camp, Alcibiades offered the Athenians some advice. He told them that Aegospotami was a poor choice for their camp. They ought to move to Sestus where they would have both a harbour and supplies; at Aegospotami they had neither. They had to bring in supplies from Sestus, which was several miles away. Alcibiades also suggested that the sailors were given too much freedom to wander away from the camp. Lysander was just across the strait with an abundance of supplies and a crew who stood constantly ready to obey his command. Alcibiades' advice, as usual, was perspicacious. On the next day the Athenians at Aegospotami, who apparently chose a leading general each day on a rotating basis, were under the command of Philocles. Philocles set out with a squadron of thirty triremes. Lysander attacked the squadron, and, when Philocles returned to the base, the Spartans pursued him there. The other Athenians were not prepared for attack and were easily defeated.[148] The question remains why Philocles set out with only thirty of the 180 triremes.[149] Either Philocles had decided to take the advice of Alcibiades and retreat to Sestus,[150] or he initiated a naval strategy that went awry.[151] Whatever their motivation, the Athenians suffered their final defeat at Aegospotami. This battle brought on the end of the Peloponnesian War and the collapse of the Athenian Empire.

After the battle Lysander sailed away to take control of several states and then to invest the city of Athens. Alcibiades knew that he was no longer safe as a resident in the Thracian Chersonese. He left many of his possessions behind him and moved into the interior of Thrace.[152] The Thracians took advantage of Alcibiades' misfortune and relieved him of most of the rest of his belongings. He then apparently took refuge with Pharnabazus who gave him the Phrygian city of Grynium from which he received revenue.[153]

Alcibiades conceived a plan to go to the Great King. Perhaps he reasoned that, with Athens out of the way, Sparta and Persia would eventually come into conflict over the disposition of western Asia Minor. Darius II died in 405[154] and was succeeded by his son Artaxerxes II (405–358), the older brother of Cyrus (b. 424?). It is possible that Alcibiades became aware of Cyrus' intention to take the throne for himself and planned to use that information in order to gain influence with Artaxerxes.[155]

There are differing accounts of the murder of Alcibiades (404).[156] If his death is a mystery, there are many suspects: Critias and the Thirty Tyrants of Athens, Agis, Lysander or other Spartans, Tissaphernes, Pharnabazus, and Cyrus. All these men could reasonably have wanted to see Alcibiades dead. However, there are enough details in common in the sources to suggest a core of truth. Only Justin says that Alcibiades was actually killed by agents of the Thirty Tyrants. This is the least plausible explanation. There can be little doubt that the Thirty wished Alcibiades dead, but they did not have the means to kill him, and their influence on Lysander was probably minimal. The sources stress the roles of Lysander and Pharnabazus. Xenophon, as was stated in the Preface, failed even to mention the death of Alcibiades. Diodorus (specifically citing Ephorus) emphasizes that Pharnabazus killed Alcibiades for reasons of his own. Alcibiades, according to this version, learned of Cyrus' plan to rebel against his brother. He took this information to the court of Pharnabazus and requested an audience with Artaxerxes so that he could be the first to inform the king of his brother's intentions. Pharnabazus decided that he should be the one to inform

Artaxerxes and so refused Alcibiades' request. Alcibiades, according to Diodorus, decided to make the same request to the satrap of Paphlagonia and set out in that direction. Pharnabazus, fearing that Alcibiades would be the first to reach the Great King with the news, sent out men with orders to kill him. These men found him in a village in Phrygia where he had stopped for the night. They set the place on fire, and when Alcibiades tried to escape, the men killed him with their javelins. This is not a wholly convincing story. If Pharnabazus' motive was simply to get information to Artaxexes before Alcibiades, he could have sent a message that would have arrived long before the Athenian. Even if he had gone himself, he, undoubtedly, could have arranged a meeting with the Great King before Alcibiades, who would have had many more obstacles in his path. Alcibiades would have to go to Paphlagonia, persuade the satrap there to let him pass, make arrangements for a guide, if successful with the satrap, and then wait for an audience with Artaxerxes. Also, it seems likely that, if Alcibiades had learned of Cyrus' rebellion, Pharnabazus, with far greater resources, would have heard of it too.

According to Nepos, the idea of killing Alcibiades began with Critias and others of the Thirty Tyrants. They threatened Lysander to the effect that, if he did not deal with Alcibiades, he would have trouble in Athens. Lysander, apparently convinced by these threats, demanded that Pharnabazus deliver Alcibiades alive or dead. Lysander threatened that, if the satrap did not deliver Alcibiades, the Spartans would renounce their alliance with the Great King. Pharnabazus, according to Nepos, reluctantly sent two men, Susamithres and Bagaeus, to kill Alcibiades, who was waiting in Phrygia to leave on his mission to Artaxerxes. In this version, Alcibiades was accompanied by an unnamed friend from Arcadia. The assassins, as in Diodorus, drove him out into the open by setting the place on fire and then felled him with spears. They decapitated him and took his head to Pharnabazus. An unnamed woman, who used to live with him, cremated his body in the fire set by the assassins.

Plutarch also begins his account by saying that Critias complained to Lysander that Alcibiades alive was a threat to the government of the Thirty Tyrants. However, in Plutarch's version, Critias failed to convince him. The Spartans ordered Lysander to put Alcibiades to death either because they too feared that Alcibiades was a threat to the Athenian oligarchy or because of the personal animosity of Agis. Lysander, in turn, ordered Pharnabazus to kill Alcibiades, and Pharnabazus enlisted

Sousamithras, his uncle, and Magaeus (not Bagaeus as in Nepos), his brother, to perform the deed.

Alcibiades, as in the other versions, was in a small town in Phrygia. However, in Plutarch's account, he was accompanied by the hetaira Timandra, who might be the woman Nepos mentions but does not name. Timandra was the mother of Lais, believed to be the most beautiful courtesan of her era.[157] Mother and daughter, if there is any truth to this anecdote, were from the Sicilian city of Hyccara. Nicias sacked that city shortly after Alcibiades was recalled in 415 and sold its population into slavery.[158] According to Plutarch, Lais, still a young girl, was sold at that time and carried away to the Peloponnese.[159] Whatever her historicity, Timandra performs the same function in this version as the unnamed woman did in Nepos. Alcibiades is not beheaded here except in a dream he had shortly before his assassination. Otherwise, this episode is similar to the other accounts. Plutarch, however, records an alternative version that has nothing to do with politics. Alcibiades had seduced a girl from a prominent family and had taken her with him. The brothers of this girl, in Plutarch's second version, burned his house and killed him with spears.

Although this alternative version is not difficult to believe, the most probable scenario is that Lysander, either on his own or ordered by the Spartan government, demanded that Pharnabazus kill Alcibiades. Pharnabazus appointed two men to carry out the deed, the men set fire to Alcibiades' hut and impaled him with spears as he attempted to escape. They probably did take his head back to Pharnabazus as proof that they had accomplished their goal.

## Conclusion

Cornelius Nepos said of Alcibiades that no one ever exceeded him either in his faults or in his virtues.[160] Although this statement is certainly an exaggeration, it has a kernel of truth. The career of Alcibiades forms a fitting coda to the history of Greece in the fifth century, a period of enormous creativity in every field of human endeavour, and yet a civilization apparently bent on self-destruction. Alcibiades' intelligence was directed toward the field of military strategy. This is not the aspect of the Greek mind that we admire most today, but is was one on which Alcibiades' contemporaries placed great emphasis. Alcibiades was one of Athens' great military strategists and deserves to be mentioned in the same company as Themistocles and Cimon. His accomplishments include the creation of an anti-Spartan league in the heart of the Peloponnese and his masterly victories at Cyzicus, Chalcedon, and Byzantium. No other Athenian general of his generation had the same combination of charisma, daring, and intelligence.

It is useless to speculate on what Alcibiades might have done had he lived. The truth is that he had made too many enemies. He probably would have found it difficult to re-enter Athenian politics after the war, not only because of past quarrels and suspicions but also because he had become something of a symbol of an extravagant and arrogant Athenian imperialism. After the war Athens would have to face a different kind of reality. She would have to act with diplomacy and subtlety. She would have to deal with Spartan leaders and Persian satraps who had come to distrust Alcibiades profoundly. Athens would need smaller men to negotiate in an era of reduced possibilities. She could no longer afford Alcibiades, who had become to other nations, as well, the symbol of a revived and unrepentant Athens. Neither the Spartans nor the Persians wanted to see Athens revive again so soon. Alcibiades' hope that Artaxerxes might set him up as a rival to the Spartans was one of the few plans of his that was unrealistic and that had no hope of realization.

All this is hindsight. Alcibiades could not have known that he was already an anachronism. He had risen from the flames more than once, and he was still a young man. At about forty-five, he might well expect to have his best years ahead of him. He knew that the days of the Thirty were limited, since Athens did not tolerate oligarchy for long, and that she had no other leader of his stature or ability. He was right in expecting an eventual rift between Sparta and Persia, but this would not happen in time to save him. For the moment he was the common target of leaders from Sparta, Persia, and Athens. Alcibiades died as he had lived, in the midst of a whirlwind of events: vital, controversial, admired, and hated, and trying once again to become his country's leader.

# Appendix

# Alcibiades, Genos, and Eupatridae

It is sometimes alleged that Alcibiades belonged to the genos Eupatridae [e.g. J. Toepffer, *RE s.v.* 'Alkibiades' (2) 1516; Hatzfeld 3]. Both of these terms, 'genos' and 'Eupatrid', are the centres of complex controversies that are far from settled. Both are ordinary Greek words with ordinary definitions, but over the years they have acquired specialized meanings. Let us begin with 'genos' (pl.=gene). *LSJ* defines γένος as race, offspring, clan, and family. Other Greek states had 'gene', but our evidence comes mainly from Athens. Over the last century, historians have created an elaborate and technical interpretation of the Athenian gene. Although there were differences among historians on certain points, there was a growing consensus. J. Toepffer's *Attische Genealogie* (Berlin 1889) was a milestone in this process. Toepffer catalogued what he considered known Athenian gene (including the Alcmaeonids and the Eupatridae) and assumed, since there was no evidence for lower-class membership in the Athenian gene, that they were restricted to the nobility. This assumption has found wide support [E. Meyer, *Geschichte des Altertums*[5] (1954) 278; *HAC* 67; *OCD*[2] 462]. Other Greek states apparently did not observe this restriction and even created new gene for their lower classes (*OCD*[2] 461). Other characteristics of Athenian gene were thought to include descent from a common mythical ancestor [P.J. Rhodes, *A Commentary on the Aristotelian Athenaion Politeia* (Oxford 1981) 69] and maintenance of a cult (*HAC* 65; *OCD*[2] 461–2). Membership was traced in the male line only, from father to son (Wade-Gery 87). Felix Bourriot [*Recherches sur la nature du génos* (Lille 1976)] has attacked this traditional view in a massive book (over 1,400 pages) that demands serious consideration. Bourriot argues that 'genos' was a commonplace Greek word that never truly carried the highly technical sense that historians have given it. Bourriot does not deny the existence of the genos, but he claims that it meant

99

different things to different generations. At the time of Alcibiades the term 'genos' was applied only to the sacerdotal families. Alcibiades, he argues, like many of Athens' leaders, did not belong to a genos. I believe that Bourriot is right, but the debate will continue. It may take another generation to reach a new consensus on the meaning of genos.

The debate on the Eupatridae centres on the question of whether they were a class or a genos. Some historians believe that there was a hereditary class of nobles in early Athens (based mainly on Ar. *AP* 13.2 and Plut, *Thes*. 25.2) called the Eupatridae. They dominated the politics and religion of Athens until their powers were gradually reduced by a series of reformers beginning with Solon (Rhodes, op. cit. 74–6). It has also been suggested that the Eupatridae consisted of the collected gene (Wade-Gery 86–115; $OCD^2$ s.v. 'genos'). Other scholars argue that the Eupatridae were a single genos. There is good evidence that there was, in fact, a genos Eupatridae in the Hellenistic period and later (Polemon *ap. schol.* Soph. *Oed. Col.* 489). There is not, however, any compelling evidence for a genos Eupatridae in the fifth century. Hatzfeld argued that there was both a Eupatrid class and a Eupatrid genos (3–8). Most scholars have argued for the existence of the class to disprove the genos, or for the genos to disprove the class. The view adopted here is that the Eupatridae were neither a hereditary class nor a genos in the classical era.

Three passages are most often discussed in connection with this problem: Isocrates 16.25, Plato's *I Alcibiades* 121a, and [Plutarch] *Vit. X Or.* 834b. The passage in Isocrates' speech *De Bigis* is: ὁ γὰρ πατὴρ πρὸς μέν ἀνδρῶν ἦν Εὐπατριδῶν, ὧν τὴν εὐγένειαν ἐξ αὐτῆς τῆς ἐπωνυμίας ῥᾴδιον γνῶναι, πρὸς γυναικῶν δ'Ἀλκμεωνιδῶν. ('My father [Alcibiades' son is speaking] on the male side was one of the Eupatridae, the nobility of which one can easily know from the name itself, on the female side, Alcmaeonid.'). Many have argued that this passage proves that Alcibiades belonged to a genos Eupatridae [U. v. Wilamowitz-Moellendorff, *Hermes* 22 (1887), 121 n.1; Toepffer (1889) op. cit. 479–83; Hatzfeld 3; F. Jacoby (1949) *Atthis* 263, n. 156). J.K. Davies seems much closer to the mark when he says that Isocrates was simply using the term as 'a sign of the inherited distinction of Alcibiades' (Davies, *APF* 12). Isocrates was probably only saying that Alcibiades came from a noble family on his father's side and from the famous Alcmaeonids on his mother's side. R. Sealey says that by placing these two names together, Isocrates implied that the Eupatridae were a genos [*A*

*History of the Greek City States* (Berkeley and Los Angeles 1976)
117; see also *Essays in Greek Politics* (New York 1967) 30–4,
30–41]. This seems an unnecessarily technical interpretation.
Even without considering Bourriot's objections, the status of the
Alcmaeonids as a genos, with all the trappings of cult and
mythical eponym, is in doubt (see Wade-Gery 106–7; Davies,
*APF* 369–70).

The second passage used to defend the genos Eupatridae is *I
Alcibiades* 121a. This passage says nothing about Eupatridae, but
in it Alcibiades does claim to belong to a genos that went back to
Eurysaces, and through Eurysaces to Zeus. Eurysaces was the
son of Telamonian Aias, the more famous Greek hero of that
name, and the greatest warrior, after Achilles, against the
Trojans (Hom. *Il.* 2.768–9). He was named after his father's
shield (Soph. *Aj.* 574–5). Plutarch (*Sol.* 10.3) relates the
Athenian tradition that Eurysaces and his half-brother Philaeus
gave the island of Salamis to Athens in return for Athenian
citizenship. Eurysaces took up residence at Melite. The genos to
which Alcibiades belonged may be that of the Salaminioi [see
Wade-Gery, *Essays* 106–10; W.S. Ferguson, *Hesperia* 7 (1938)
1–74; Davies, *APF* 10–12). There is an inscription that ties the
Salaminioi to the worship of Eurysaces (Ferguson, op. cit.). And
yet there is still room for doubt. Bourriot looks at the context of
this allusion and is unconvinced (op. cit. 396–401). Socrates is
suggesting that noble races (gene) produce better natures. He
goes on to say that the genos of the Spartan kings goes back to
Hercules and the genos of the Persian kings goes back to
Achaemenes, and both of these go back to Zeus. Alcibiades says
that his goes back to Eurysaces and from there to Zeus. Socrates
then says that he is of the genos of Daedalus. This is a playful
statement that few would take seriously. Daedalus was the
mythical inventor of sculpture, the hereditary occupation of
Socrates' family. [For a different view, see A.E. Taylor, *Socrates*
(London 1951) 40–1.] What would happen, Socrates continues, if
you had to go to Persia and to prove your nobility to them? And
haven't you noticed, he inquires further, how the Spartans keep
their queens under such strict protection to prevent them from
diluting their nobility by giving birth to a child by anyone other
than the king? All this, Bourriot argues, sounds too much like
what really did happen to Alcibiades later in his life. Bourriot
speculates that Alcibiades appropriated Eurysaces as his ancestor
to impress the Spartans and the Persians with his noble lineage
(op. cit. 423). This conclusion may be fanciful, but Bourriot's
illumination of this passage does cast doubt on the definitive

attribution of a genos, in the traditional sense, to Alcibiades. The passage is too playful, and the uses of the word 'genos' are too vague, to inspire absolute confidence.

The third passage, from [Plutarch] *Lives of the Ten Orators*, is ambiguous at best: Ἀνδοκίδης . . . γένους εὐπατριδῶν, ὡς δ᾽ Ἑλλάνικος καὶ ᾽απὸ Ἑρμοῦ, καθήκει γὰρ εἰς αὐτὸν τὸ κηρύκων γένος. ('Andocides [was] of noble birth and according to Hellanicus even from Hermes, for the genos Kerykes goes back to him.'). The author seems to be saying that Andocides belonged to the genos Kerykes. γένους εὐπατριδῶν may mean something other than 'of noble birth', but it is not proof of the existence of a genos Eupatridae in classical Athens. Andocides could not belong to two gene.

# Chronological table
# (all dates are BC)

| | |
|---|---|
| c.450 | Birth of Alcibiades |
| 446 | Death of Alcibiades' father, Cleinias, at the battle of Coronea |
| 432 | Revolt of Potidaea |
| 431–404 | Peloponnesian War |
| 430/429 | The siege of Potidaea ends |
| 425/424 | Alcibiades is a member of the commission to reassess the tribute |
| 424 | Battle of Delium |
| 421 | Peace of Nicias |
| 420 | Argive or Quadruple Alliance of Athens, Argos, Elis, and Mantinea |
| 418 | Battle of Mantinea |
| 416 | The ostracism of Hyperbolus. Alcibiades enters seven chariot teams in the Olympic games |
| 415 | The Sicilian expedition. The mutilation of the herms. Alcibiades is recalled |
| 414–412 | Alcibiades in Sparta |
| 413 | The Sicilian expedition ends in disaster for the Athenians |
| 412 | The revolt of Chios, Miletus, and other Athenian allies |
| 412/411 | Alcibiades takes refuge with Tissaphernes |
| 411 | The government of the 400 at Athens. Alcibiades is recalled by the Athenian fleet at Samos. The battle of Abydus |
| 410 | Battle of Cyzicus |
| 408 | Battles of Chalcedon and Byzantium |
| 407 | Alcibiades returns to Athens |
| 406 | Alcibiades is deposed after the battle of Notium |
| 405 | Alcibiades lives in the Thracian Chersonese |
| 404 | Death of Alcibiades in Phrygia |

# Notes

**Chapter one    Family, youth, and early influences**

1 All dates are BC unless otherwise noted. For a discussion of the year of Alcibiades' birth, see Davies, *APF* 18.
2 Citizens were, of course, free adult males. The entire population including women, slaves, and resident aliens was probably between 200,000 and 400,000. Cf. A.W. Gomme, *The Population of Athens* (Oxford 1933); N.G.L. Hammond, *A History of Greece*, 3rd edn (Oxford 1986) 328–30. The citizen population of Athens in 431 was about 40,000. This figure is a reasonable inference from Thuc. 2.13.6–7 and has recently been defended by M. H. Hansen [*AJAH* 7 (1982) 172–89].
3 Plut. *Alc*. 1.6–8.
4 Paus. 2.18.9.
5 Kastor v. Rhodos, *FGrH* 250 F4.
6 See *Die Chronik des Eusebios*, Josef Kaerst (ed.) (Leipzig 1911) 92.
7 Thuc. 1.126.
8 Plut. *Sol*. 12.1.
9 Thuc. 1.126.
10 Ar. *AP* 1; Plut. *Sol*. 12.
11 So W.G. Forrest, *BCH* 80 (1956) 41.
12 Plut. *Sol*. 12.2.
13 Hdt. 6.125.
14 Plut. *Sol*. 11.2.
15 Aeschin. 3.107–12; *schol*. Pind. *Nem*. 9; Paus.10.7.4–6.
16 R. Sealey, *A History of the Greek City States* (Berkeley and Los Angeles 1976) 47; Forrest, op. cit. 33.
17 Pind. *Pyth*. 7.14–15 and *schol*.
18 Davies, *APF* 371; Forrest, op. cit. 51.
19 Forrest, ibid.
20 M.F. McGregor, *TAPA* 72 (1941) 276.
21 Hdt. 1.61.
22 B.D. Meritt, *Hesperia* 8 (1939) 59–65.
23 Hdt. 5.66,70.
24 Hdt. 5.73; E.M. Walker, in *CAH* 5.158.
25 Aelian *VH* 12.24.

26  Hdt. 6.123.

27  Davies, *APF* 379.

28  Plut. *Alc*. 1.1; Isoc. 16.28; Plat. I *Alc*. 112c. For a discussion of the date in relation to other events of the Pentakontaetia, see A.W. Gomme, *HCT* 1 (1945) 389–413.

29  Isoc. 16.25.

30  Plut. *Alc*. 1.1.

31  W. Dittenberger, *Hermes* 37 (1902) 1–13.

32  E. Vanderpool, *Hesperia* 21 (1952) 1–8.

33  Lys. 14.39.

34  [Andoc.] 4.34. Lysias and [Andocides] say that Alcibiades II was ostracized twice. This is probably not true. For discussions of this problem, see Hatzfeld 14–15, 20–2; A.E. Raubitschek, *TAPA* 79 (1948) 203. The use of square brackets denotes an item commonly included among the works of an ancient author but no longer considered to have been written by him (i.e. pseudo-Andocides, etc.).

35  Thuc. 5.43.2.

36  This idea was also suggested by Hatzfeld 16–17.

37  Thuc. 1.101–3.

38  *HCT* 1.395, 411–412.

39  Vanderpool, op. cit. 4.

40  Isoc. 16.26.

41  A.E. Raubitschek, *RhM* 98 (1955) 258–62; P. Bicknell, *MPhL* 1 (1975) 51–64.

42  Hdt. 6.131.2; Davies, *APF* 379.

43  Isoc. 16.26. There is no compelling reason to reject this information no matter how wary we may be of the reliability of Isocrates as a source. The existence of Alcibiades I is accepted by Davies (*APF* 15) and by virtually all scholars who have written on the subject.

44  Correct Hatzfeld's unusual slip on 12, where he calls it the battle of Eurymedon.

45  Hdt. 8.17.

46  Davies, *APF* 15, 51–2.

47  And a daughter, see Davies, *APF* 17.

48  H.B. Mattingly has led the fight against dating the decree at this time. He favours a much later date (426/425). See *Historia* 10 (1961) 150–69; *BSA* 65 (1970) 129–33.

49  Andoc. 1.16.

50  So Davies, *APF* 18.

51  Ibid.

52  Nep. *Alc*. 2.1.

53  Davies, *APF* 18, n.1.

54  Beloch, 1.151–2; Miltner, *RE s.v.* 'Perikles' 754.

55  The idea that Pericles worked for Cimon's ostracism is implied in Plut. *Per*. 9.5 and is a reasonable inference from the facts that he was a rival and that he had been one of Cimon's prosecutors in 463. (Ar. *AP* 27.1; Plut. *Per*. 10.6).

56  *HCT* 1.306–7.

57 So C.M. Bowra, *Periclean Athens* (New York 1971) 47.
58 So *HAC* 254.
59 Plut. *Per*. 10.4–5; *HAC* 255; R. Sealey, *Essays In Greek Politics* (New York 1967) 63–4.
60 For example Thuc. 2.65: 'Athens, though in name a democracy, gradually became in fact a government ruled by its first citizen.'
61 For a discussion of how the Megarian Decree was 'an extreme demonstration of Athenian imperialism', see R. Meiggs, *The Athenian Empire* (Oxford 1972) 203.
62 Plut. *Per*. 18.2.
63 'We can be virtually certain, by analogy with other pre-industrial societies, that well over half, perhaps even 90 percent, of the adult population (slave or free, man or woman) will have been engaged in agriculture' [J.K. Davies, *Democracy and Classical Greece* (Stanford, Cal. 1983) 22].
64 Davies (op. cit. 36) finds no 'context in classical Greek history where a "middle class" in any sense (most plausibly small landed proprietors, never in a professional or entrepreneurial sense) exercised a specific interest and pressure of its own rather than being assimilated to the value-system either of "the few" or of "the many"'.
65 Hdt. 5.66.
66 R. Sealey [*Hermes* 84 (1956) 234–47] argues that Pericles did not stand for any consistent political policies but was primarily interested in 'personal and family-friendships' (246). Sealey rejects the testimony of Thucydides, Aristotle, and Plutarch and offers instead only a series of propositions that contain the word 'perhaps.' I am reluctant to accept Sealey's conclusions without more convincing evidence.
67 Thuc. 2.35–46.
68 Ar. *AP* 27.1. Pericles' attitude seems clear even if the nature of his reform of the Areopagus does not. For other references to the relationship between democracy and the navy, see P.J. Rhodes, *A Commentary on the Aristotelian Athenaion Politeia* (Oxford 1981) 336–7.
69 Ar. *AP* 27.2–4.
70 Plut. *Per*. 9.1.
71 Ibid.
72 Thuc. 2.65.9.
73 Thuc. 2.65.3; Plut. *Per*. 35.4.
74 Sealey (1956) op. cit. 246.
75 Plut. *Per*. 12–14.
76 Thuc. 2.41.4 and 1.127.3.
77 M.I. Finley, *Democracy Ancient and Modern* (London 1985) 87.
78 Finley, ibid. 85.
79 Thuc. 5.43.2.
80 Thuc. 6.89–92.
81 Thuc. 5.26.5.

82  Thuc. 6.89.3–4. Trans. R. Warner, in *The Peloponnesian War* (Harmondsworth 1954) 467.
83  Thuc. 6.89.6.
84  Alcibiades also flirted briefly with oligarchy in 411 (Thuc. 8.47). This flirtation, however, was short-lived and was undoubtedly motivated by his desire to be recalled to Athens. This incident will be discussed in more detail in Chapter 5.
85  For the similarity of Alcibiades' ideas on imperialism to those of Pericles, as expressed in Thucydides, see J. de Romilly, *Thucydides and Athenian Imperialism* (New York 1979) 210. See also A.W. Gomme [*JHS* 71 (1951) 70–80 reprinted in *More Essays in Greek History and Literature* (Oxford 1962) 92–111] who says of Alcibiades that 'his speech in advocacy of the expedition to Sicily has much in it of Pericles', and who concludes that Cleon and Alcibiades 'were the principal heirs to Perikles' policy'.
86  Thuc. 5.16.1.
87  Thuc. 6.89.4–5.
88  Isoc. 8.126; 15.234. See also Ar. *AP* 27.1.
89  W.R. Connor, *The New Politicians of Fifth-Century Athens* (Princeton, NJ 1971) 3, 109–10. For Aristophanes and Thucydides the word and the concept had negative associations. For a discussion of this idea, see Manfred Lossau, *Politeia und Res Publica . . . dem Andenken R. Starks gewidmet* (Wiesbaden 1969) 83–8. Thucydides only uses the word twice, once for Cleon (4.21.3) and once for Androcles (8.65.2).
90  M.I. Finley, *Past and Present* 21 (1962) 4.
91  G.E.M. de Ste Croix has suggested that the traditional view of the 'demagogue' is unrealistic. See *The Class Struggle in the Ancient Greek World* (Ithaca 1981) 290. He distinguishes the Greek word from our word by the use of the inverted commas, *The Origins of the Peloponnesian War* (London 1972) 359, n.4.
92  Connor, op. cit. 134. See also Davies (1983) op. cit. 113–14. In commenting on Plut. *Per.* 13.13, he discusses Pericles' 'populist instinct for the melodramatic gesture'.
93  Thuc. 3.36.6. M.L. Lang's attempt [*CP* 67 (1972) 159–169] to prove that Cleon was an oligarch in disguise is not convincing.
94  Plut. *Per.* 39.2.
95  Connor, op. cit. 140–1, shows the similarity of Alcibiades and Cleon in two passages, one from Plutarch and one from Thucydides. Both are attacks on Nicias. They have a curiously similar tone.
96  See Finley (1962) op. cit. 22–3; Connor, op. cit. 139–43.
97  Ar. *AP* 28.4.
98  Connor, op. cit. 151–73. See also Davies (1983) op. cit. 114.
99  Connor, op. cit. 151–4.
100 Thuc. 8.65.2.
101 *HAC* 260–84.
102 Plut. *Alc.* 1.3.
103 Thuc. 5.43.2.

104 Vanderpool, op. cit. 7–8.
105 Thuc. 8.6.3.
106 Ibid.
107 Plat. *Prot.* 320a.
108 See Davies, *APF* 18, who calls him a 'psychotic delinquent'.
109 Plat. *I Alc.* 118e.
110 Plut. *Alc.* 3.1.
111 Cited by Athenaeus 12.525b.
112 No commentator, to my knowledge, accepts this fragment as being from one of Antiphon's genuine orations. B. Perrin [*Plutarch's Nicias and Alcibiades* (New York 1912) 262] is typical: 'It was in all probability a fabrication, by some unknown sophist, dating from about the middle of the fourth century B.C., when the growing cult of Alcibiades' memory roused much hostile literary activity.' See also Hatzfeld 59–60.
113 So R.J. Littman, *TAPA* 101 (1970) 264.
114 Hatzfeld 30.
115 Plut. *Alc.* 2.3–4.
116 Plut. *Alc.* 9.
117 Plut. *Alc.* 2.2–3.
118 Plat. *I Alc.* 122b; Plut. *Alc.* 1.3.
119 Plut. *Per.* 4.1–4.
120 The aulos is frequently translated as a 'flute', but this is wrong since it was a reed, or possibly a double-reed, instrument (*OCD*$^2$ 710).
121 Plat. *I Alc.* 106e; Plut. *Alc.* 2.5–7.
122 Plut. *Alc.* 2.7.
123 Plut. *Alc.* 4.4–6; *Mor.* 762c; Athen. 12.534e–f. There are slight variations. See also Perrin, op. cit. 264.
124 Littman, op. cit. 268.
125 Plut. *Alc.* 5.
126 Littman, op. cit. 269.
127 D.A. Russell notes the symmetry in *PCPS* 12 (1966) 40.
128 As D.A. Russell notes, the story implies that Alcibiades had control over his own property, and so must have been an adult. See his *Plutarch* (London 1973) 118.
129 Athen. 5.220c.
130 Diog. Laert. 1.15; 6.13.
131 Athen. 5.220c. The fragments of Aeschines were collected with commentary by H. Dittmar [Philolische Untersuchungen 21 (1912)].
132 Athen. 12.525b. This is apparently the same abusive oration that told the story of Democrates mentioned above. It also alleged that Alcibiades killed an attendant in the palaestra of Sibyrtius. See Plut. *Alc.* 3.
133 Athen. 12.534f–535a; Athen. 13.574e = Lysias Fr. 246 (Thalheim).
134 So Littman, op. cit. 268, 275.
135 See Plut. *Alc.* 1.4.
136 For the best discussion of Greek homosexuality, see K.J. Dover, *Greek Homosexuality* (Cambridge, Mass. 1978).

137 Plat. *I Alc.* 131c–d.
138 A.E. Taylor, *Socrates* (London 1951) 46–8.
139 The date of Agathon's victory can be found in Athenaeus 217b. Many scholars continue to place it a year later on the eve of the Sicilian expedition. See K.J. Dover (ed.) *Plato: Symposium* (Cambridge 1980) 9–10, n.1, who dates it to 416.
140 Seth L. Schein attempts to prove that Plato had a political goal in presenting this scene [*Theta-Pi* 3 (1974) 158–67]. Alcibiades, in his view, was a symbol of the imperialistic policies of Athens in the fifth century whose leaders were examples 'of loving appetitively, irrationally, in the wrong way' (166). These views are not inconsistent with Plato's philosophy but would seem to be secondary in a dialogue whose primary concern is the variety of human love. But Schein is quite right when he notes that Plato was 'fundamentally antipathetic' (167) to Alcibiades in spite of the considerable charm with which he imbues his portrait.
141 Dover (1980) op. cit. 164–5.
142 Plat. *Symp.* 216b–c.
143 Xen. *Mem.* 1.2.12–16.
144 Littman, op. cit. 263–76.
145 Littman cites Athenaeus 5.219b–220a. Athenaeus does not actually say that they were lovers, but only that Socrates pursued Alcibiades with carnal intentions. Still, this is quite different from the picture Plato draws in the *Symposium*.
146 As recorded in Diog. Laert. 4.49.
147 Littman, op. cit. 275.
148 Plat. *Symp.* 215e.
149 To which we may add the fragments of Aeschines the Socratic collected by Dittmar, op. cit., and Aristophanes' comic portrait in the *Clouds*.
150 Taylor, op. cit. 28–9.
151 Charles H. Kahn [*CQ* n.s. 31 (1981) 305–20] does not doubt that the early dialogues reveal a historically accurate portrait of Socrates, but he concludes that 'the doctrines and arguments contained in them [the dialogues] . . . belong to Plato and to the fourth century' (320).
152 Xen. *Mem.* 4.4.9. Trans. E.C. Marchant, *Memorabilia and Oeconomicus* (New York 1923) 313.
153 Taylor, op. cit. 70–83.
154 *HCT* 4.246.

**Chapter two    Alcibiades and the early stages of the Peloponnesian War**

1 Diodorus (12.38.3), in an anecdote that he took from Ephorus, accused Alcibiades of being the chief instigator of the war. This anecdote, undoubtedly apocryphal, implies that Pericles was an embezzler and that Alcibiades cynically suggested the war to Pericles as a means of escaping notice for his wrongdoing. Plutarch (*Alc.* 7.3)

gives us a milder version of the story in which Pericles is not so obviously an embezzler.

2 Alcibiades in Plato's *I Alcibiades* had already decided on a political career in 432 at the age of eighteen. The idea that Alcibiades would already have chosen such a career does not seem surprising considering his family, his position as the ward of Pericles, and his obvious ambition.

3 The Corinthians claimed victory, but since they retreated and refused to resume the conflict, it is fair to say that they lost. Thuc. 1.50–4.

4 The basic narrative of the Potidaean campaign comes from Thucydides 1.56–65 and 2.66–70. Alcibiades' participation in the campaign is known primarily from Plato's *Symposium* 219e–220e.

5 Thuc.1.58.1. The Spartans promised to invade Attica if the Athenians attacked Potidaea, a promise they did not keep.

6 A.W. Gomme [*HCT* 1.222–4, 421–5 and in *CR* 55 (1941) 59–67] believed the revolt was earlier, in April of 432, but he is in a decided minority on this point. In the uncertainty over the Athenian calendar, it would be unwise to press too insistently for precise Julian dates, but I agree with the majority of historians [Beloch 2.219–22; W. Kolbe, *Thukydides im Lichte der Urkunden* (Stuttgart 1930) 1–49; H.T. Wade-Gery, *JHS* 53 (1933) 135–6] who place the battle of Potidaea in or around September 432. W.E. Thompson [*Hermes* 96 (1968) 216–232] places the battle in October, but this is only a minor variation.

7 Isoc. 16.29. The problem with Isocrates' statement will be discussed in the next paragraph.

8 Thuc. 1.64; Plat. *Chrm.* 153b.

9 Hatzfeld 65, n. 1.

10 R. Sealey seems to think this force was operating against Macedonia in the winter of 433/432. See *A History of the Greek City States* (Berkeley and Los Angeles 1976) 315.

11 Thuc. 1.56–60.

12 Thuc. 1.59.1.

13 *ATL* 2, list 22, col. 2, l. 70.

14 Plat. *Symp.* 219e–220b. Trans. W.R.M. Lamb (Cambridge, Mass. 1939) 233.

15 As it was by Hatzfeld 65.

16 This account of the Archidamian War comes from Thucydides unless otherwise noted.

17 Thuc. 1.23. Trans. R. Warner in *The Peloponnesian War* (Harmondsworth 1954) 49.

18 For example Bury–Meiggs: 'Within a few years this method would doubtless have been crowned with success and brought about a peace favourable to Athens, but for untoward events which he could not foresee' (253). See also N.G.L. Hammond, *A History of Greece*, 3rd edn (Oxford 1986) 348: 'Pericles' strategy involved Athens in no serious risks and gave an assurance of ultimate victory.'

19 For a negative assessment of Pericles' strategy, see K.J. Beloch, *Die*

*attische Politik seit Perikles* (Leipzig 1884) 22–24 and Beloch 1.300
and n. 1. Sealey wonders whether such a defensive policy could ever
deliver a definitive victory (op. cit. 325). D. Kagan believes that
Pericles expected a short war, and that had 'he lived he would have
had no choice but to intensify the war effort and raise the level of
Athenian military action' [*The Outbreak of the Peloponnesian War*
(Ithaca, NY 1969) 340–1].
20 Thuc. 1.144.
21 Thuc. 2.60–4.
22 Warner, op. cit. 161.
23 See, for example, J.H. Finley, *Thucydides* (Cambridge, Mass. 1942)
194: 'Presumably he would have held that, after its successful issue
and assuming a continued decline in Spartan vigor, Athens, as the
more progressive, more modern state, would inevitably gain in
influence and might someday go on to a still greater future.'
H.T. Wade-Gery (*OCD*$^2$ 1069) thought that Pericles originally
planned an offensive war and only fell back on defensive strategy
after setbacks. There is no compelling evidence for this view.
24 The battle of Delium in 424 is a notable exception.
25 Thuc. 3.36–49.
26 Plat. *Symp*. 221a–c.
27 Plat. *La*. 181 a–b.
28 Aristoph. *Ach*. 716. Aristophanes had mentioned Alcibiades two
years earlier in *The Banqueters*, a play that is not extant. The line
seems to satirize him for his refinement of speech. Frag. no. 198 in
J. Edmonds, *The Fragments of Attic Comedy* (Leiden 1957) 1.629–31.
The play has a father arguing with his profligate son in a situation
similar to *The Clouds*. The son is using jargon and fancy language,
and the father is identifying the source of his son's vocabulary. Son:
ἀποκείσεταί σοι ταῦτα πη τὰ ῥήματα· πάλιν ὁ πρεσβύτης καὶ
τοῦτο σκώπτει. Father: παρ' Ἀλκιβάδου τοῦτο τ'ἀποκείσεται.
29 [Andoc.] 4.11.
30 So Hatzfeld 68–9.
31 *IG* I$^3$ 71 = *ML* 69.
32 Gomme (*HCT* 3.500–4) is a notable exception.
33 Plut. *Alc*. 10.1–2.
34 As did Hatzfeld 69–71.
35 As Hatzfeld noted, ibid.
36 Aristoph. *Lys*. 808–20; *Av*. 1549.
37 Plut. *Alc*. 16.6 and *Ant*. 70; Lucian, *Timon or the Misanthrope*.
Shakespeare apparently based his play *Timon of Athens* on Plutarch
and Lucian.
38 Plut. *Alc*. 16.4. Pseudo-Andocides [(Andoc.) 4.17] tells,
characteristically, a more brutal version of the story in which
Agatharchus escaped after several months, and Alcibiades was left
hostile and threatening.
39 Vitr. *De Arch*. 7. Pref. 11.
40 Davies, *APF* 19.

41 Beloch 2.35; Davies, *APF* 262–3.
42 The literature on this topic is enormous. For a good introduction to the problem, see R. Meiggs, *The Athenian Empire* (Oxford 1972) 129–51, 598–9.
43 Davies, *APF* 254, 259–60.
44 Andoc. 1.130; Isoc. 16.31; Nep *Alc.* 2.1.
45 Thuc. 3.91.4.
46 Davies, *APF* 263.
47 Andoc.1.130.
48 Plat. *Prot.* 314d–e.
49 Plut. *Alc.* 8.1–3.
50 Plut. *Alc.* 8.3–6; [Andoc.] 4.13–14.
51 [Andocides] thought that Hipponicus died at the battle of Delium in 424, but probably confused him with the general, Hippocrates. See Davies, *APF* 262.
52 [Andoc.] 4.14.
53 Plut. *Alc.* 8.4.
54 Plut. *Alc.* 8.5.
55 The details of the Athenian laws and customs on divorce where the wife initiates the proceedings are not clear. [See A.R.W. Harrison, *The Law of Athens: The Family and Property* (Oxford 1968) 40–4.] A woman would have to report the case to the archon (probably the eponymous archon), but there is no evidence to indicate whether mere notification was sufficient or whether the archon would hear evidence and make a decision. Nor is there any further evidence that physical removal of the wife dissolved divorce proceedings.
56 [Andoc.] 4.14.
57 Plut. *Alc.* 8.6.
58 See n. 55.
59 Plut. *Alc.* 8.6.
60 Lys.14.28.
61 Isoc.16.45; Davies, *APF* 19.
62 So Hatzfeld 137, n. 1.
63 Isoc.16.45.
64 So Davies, *APF* 19.
65 The two speeches may have been written for the same trial and for the same offence. Lysias 14 accuses Alcibiades IV of both failing to present himself for service and of deserting the ranks. Lysias 15 makes no real distinction between the two. The second speech (15) may be only a summary of the first [so K.J. Dover, *Lysias and the Corpus Lysiacum* (Berkeley and Los Angeles 1968) 7]. Alcibiades IV seems to be primarily guilty of preferring the cavalry to the infantry and of obtaining enrolment in the former through irregular means.
66 Plut. *Alc.* 1.8, quoted in Edmonds, op. cit. 1.806, Frag. 45. Trans. B. Perrin, 5.
67 Thuc. 5.43.2; 6.89.2.
68 Hatzfeld 75.
69 Thuc. 6.89. Trans. Warner, op. cit. 467.

### Chapter three    Alcibiades and the peace of Nicias, 421–416

1  The principal source for the first two paragraphs in this chapter is
   Thuc. 5.25–48.
2  Thuc. 5.3.
3  Thuc. 5.18.
4  Thuc. 5.39.
5  Plut. *Alc*. 13.1–2. For Phaeax's mission to Italy and Sicily, see Thuc.
   5.4. For his possible participation in the ostracism of Hyperbolus,
   see Plut. *Alc*. 13.7–8.
6  Charles Fuqua [*TAPA* 96 (1965) 165–79] finds Erisistratus, Phaeax's
   father's name, among the Thirty Tyrants (Xen. *Hell*. 2.3.2).
   Assuming the name to represent Phaeax's son or cousin, he
   concludes that 'if Phaeax himself was not an oligarch, he was at
   least cognizant of their activities' (173). This association is not
   certain (see Davies, *APF* 523–24), and the conclusion is mere
   speculation.
7  This episode is narrated by Thucydides at 5.43–7.
8  Thuc. 8.6.3. The two families had been friends for several
   generations, at least since the time of Alcibiades' great-grandfather.
   The father of Endius was named Alcibiades and these two names
   alternated in their family. Thucydides says that Alcibiades was a
   Laconian name and that the Athenian family had borrowed it from
   the Spartan family, apparently as a sign of friendship.
9  Hatzfeld 89–93.
10 *HCT* 4.51–3.
11 Plut. *Alc*. 14.8–10.
12 *HCT* 4.52.
13 This conclusion seems to be supported by Alcibiades' subsequent
   treatment of the envoys as well as the location of some of the other
   emotional speeches of the recent past. Alcibiades' diatribe against
   Nicias (Plut. *Alc*. 14.4–5), Cleon's diatribe against Nicias (Thuc.
   4.27) and the 'Mytilenian Debate' (Thuc. 3.36–48) all seem to have
   taken place in the assembly.
14 So Kagan, *Peace of Nicias* 69 esp. n. 40.
15 Hatzfeld 87–93.
16 *HCT* 4.52.
17 At the opposite extreme, P.A. Brunt [*REG* 65 (1952) 59–96, esp.
   66–69] suggests that Alcibiades himself was Thucydides' informant,
   and for this reason, Alcibiades' role in this matter was greatly
   exaggerated. The possibility that Alcibiades was an informant for
   Thucydides will be discussed later in this book. Brunt is joined by
   H.D. Westlake [*Individuals in Thucydides* (Cambridge 1968)
   212–19] and E.F. Bloedow [*Alcibiades Reexamined, Historia*
   Einzelschriften Heft 21 (Wiesbaden 1973) 3–8] in his belief that
   Alcibiades had no effect in this matter. Brunt asks: 'was it not the
   diplomatic and military position that threw Athens and Argos
   together rather than the adroitness of one man?' (67). Kagan's
   answer to this question is sound, that both man and situation were

necessary, and that Alcibiades' secret message to Argos was 'vital', *Peace of Nicias* 69 n. 38.

18 This reconstruction follows that of Kagan in *Peace of Nicias* (67–74) whose interpretation seems to me the most logical.

19 Thuc. 5.43.

20 So A. Andrewes, *HCT* 4.50.

21 Kagan (*Peace of Nicias* 70) sees this as 'possible'; M.F. McGregor [*Phoenix* 19 (1965) 29 n. 8] sees it as 'quite likely'; and R.B. Kebric's entire article [*Mnemosyne* 29 (1976) 72–8] is devoted to the possibilities.

22 Kebric, op. cit. 76.

23 Thuc. 5.36.

24 Thuc. 6.16. Trans. R. Warner, in *The Peloponnesian War* (Harmondsworth 1954) 420.

25 Thuc. 6.48.

26 Thuc. 5.49–50.

27 Thuc. 5.51.

28 *HCT* 4.69.

29 Plut. *Alc.* 15.6. Trans. B. Perrin, in *Plutarch's Nicias and Alcibiades* (New York 1912) 39.

30 So Hatzfeld 98–99; and J.K. Anderson [*BSA* 49 (1954) 84]. Gomme objected to the phrase 'completely command the entrance,' but Andrewes, commenting on Gomme, thought that the Athenians 'could exercise so much control that "command" is not a great exaggeration' (*HCT* 4.70).

31 Hatzfeld 98–9. Hatzfeld pointed to Thuc. 1.111 for Pericles and Thuc. 4.21 for Cleon.

32 Kagan, *Peace of Nicias* 79.

33 Thuc. 5.53.

34 Kagan, *Peace of Nicias* 82–4.

35 Ibid. 83–4.

36 Thuc. 5.54.

37 So Andrewes, op. cit. 4.72.

38 Some scholars think that Alcibiades was elected general in 418/417. Thucydides simply says that Alcibiades went to Argos as an ambassador at the time of the battle of Mantinea (5.61.2). Diodorus (12.79) says that Alcibiades went to Argos ἰδιώτης, as a private citizen. It is usually assumed from this that, if Alcibiades had been elected as a general, he would have been sent to execute a policy for which he was primarily responsible. In 1930 H.T. Wade-Gery [*CQ* 24 (1930) 34 n. 2] suggested that an inscription (*IG* I$^3$ 370 = *ML* 77) could be restored to include the name of Alcibiades as one of the generals of 418/417 who received a payment from the treasurers of Athens ([Ἀλκιβιάδει Σκαμβονί]δει). This restoration was adopted by B.D. Meritt in *AFD* (160, 1.17) but not by R. Meiggs and D. Lewis or by Lewis in *IG* I$^3$. C.W. Fornara overstates the case considerably when he calls the restoration 'unexceptionable' [*The*

*Athenian Board of Generals from 501 to 404, Historia*
Einzelschriften 16 (Wiesbaden 1971) 63], but it remains a distinct
possibility. If Alcibiades was a general in 418/417, he was probably
elected later in the year to fill a vacancy (Wade-Gery, op. cit.;
Bury–Meiggs 537, n. 2). Whether or not Alcibiades was general in
418/417, it still remains likely that the Athenians had decided to
restrain his Peloponnesian policy. If Alcibiades was not allowed to
go to Mantinea as general, it probably meant that the Athenians
were uncomfortable with the idea of a full-scale land battle with the
Spartans.

39 So Kagan, *Peace of Nicias* 90, 103.
40 So Hatzfeld 103.
41 Thuc. 5.56.
42 The Spartans would probably sail close to the island of Aegina on
their way to Epidaurus. The Argives do not say whose territory was
violated, but that it was Athenian territory is the most logical
explanation and the one followed by Andrewes (op. cit. 4.77).
Kagan, however, suggested that it was Argive territory that was
crossed (*Peace of Nicias* 88).
43 The Athenians sent the helots from Cranii back to Pylos. The
Messenians and helots from Pylos had been settled at Cranii on the
island of Cephallenia as part of the negotiations carried on between
Athens and Sparta in 421. See Thuc. 5.35.7–8.
44 Busolt, 162–3; Beloch, *Die attische Politik seit Perikles* (Leipzig
1884) 53, Beloch 1.348.
45 A.W. Gomme *HCT* 4.78–9, 87–8.
46 Laches was one of the signers of the Peace of Nicias (Thuc. 5.19.2)
and of the Spartan–Athenian alliance (Thuc. 5.24.1). Nicostratus
had shared the command with Nicias on, at least, two occasions
(Thuc. 4.53.1; 4.129.2).
47 Gomme, op. cit. 4.78–9.
48 The size of the armies at Mantinea is a complex problem and cannot
be calculated exactly in spite of the information that Thucydides
offers at 5.67. Thucydides says (5.68.1–2) that the Spartan army
appeared larger, but that he could not be certain of the number.
W.J. Woodhouse [*King Agis of Sparta* (Oxford 1933) 131–46]
estimates that the Spartans enjoyed a numerical superiority of 1,760
men. More recently and perhaps more accurately, J.F. Lazenby
[*The Spartan Army* (Warminster 1985) 41–3, 128–9] concludes that
the Spartan side had from 10,000 to 11,000 men while the Athenian
allies had 10,000 or less. Lazenby's calculations are only slightly
lower than those of Andrewes (op. cit. 4.116).
49 These ideas conform with ideas expressed by Kagan, *Peace of Nicias*
esp. 142–3, 147–8, 153–5.
50 This paragraph is based on Thuc. 5.57–62.
51 As do Fuqua, op. cit. 176–7 and Kagan, *Peace of Nicias* 142–3.
52 See e.g. Beloch, (1884) op. cit. 339–40; H. Bengtson, *Griechische
Geschichte*[2] (Munich 1960) 232; Bury–Meiggs, 291.

53 Thuc. 8.73.
54 *FGrH* 115 F96b. The fragment reads in part:
&#7952;&#958;&#969;&#963;&#964;&#961;&#940;&#954;&#953;&#963;&#945;&#957; &#964;&#8056;&#957;
&#8077;&#960;&#941;&#961;&#946;&#959;&#955;&#959;&#957; &#7957;&#958; &#7956;&#964;&#951;.
55 A.G. Woodhead *Hesperia* 18 (1949) 78–83].
56 *IG* I³ 85.
57 McGregor, op. cit., 31–2, 43–6.
58 A.E. Raubitschek, *Phoenix* 9 (1955) 122–6.
59 R. Sealey, who accepts the date 415, appears to be an exception: *A History of the Greek City States* (Berkeley and Los Angeles 1976) 353. Andrewes (op. cit. 5.260–1) is sympathetic to Raubitschek's idea that the six years represent, not the time since Hyperbolus left Athens, but the time he was prominent in Athens. Andrewes rejects Raubitschek's date and his attempt to place the ostracism within the context of the Sicilian expedition. Raubitschek's theory is related to his acceptance of [Andoc.] 4 as a genuine fifth-century document; See *TAPA* 79 (1948) 191–210. This idea is unlikely and has been widely rejected. See e.g. K.J. Dover, *HCT* 4.287.
60 Fuqua, op. cit.
61 It has been accepted by Andrewes (op. cit. 5.261) and Kagan (*Peace of Nicias* 145).
62 Thuc. 8.73.
63 Plut. *Ar*. 7.
64 Plut. *Nic*. 11.
65 Plut. *Alc*. 13.
66 So Kagan, *Peace of Nicias* 147.
67 Plut. *Nic*. 11.7 = Plut. *Alc*. 13.15, quoted in J. Edmonds, *The Fragments of Attic Comedy* (Leiden 1957) 1.550, Frag. no 187. Trans. I. Scott-Kilvert, *Plutarch: The Rise and Fall of Athens* (Harmondsworth 1960) 222, 255.
68 Plut. *Nic*. 11.1.
69 Grote 5.504.
70 Aristotle (*AP* 43.5) tells us that the vote to hold an ostracism was held in the sixth prytany. If there was to be an actual ostracism, it would take place in the eighth prytany (*FGrH* Phil. 328 F30 and commentary).
71 Andrewes (op. cit. 5.261–4) has suggested a similar scheme although he states that Hyperbolus initiated the ostracism. Andrewes also believes that Alcibiades 'lost his nerve', and that the 'stab in the back' to Hyperbolus cost Alcibiades dearly and caused many 'good democrats' to distrust him.
72 Thuc. 5.83.4. For the date and for the suggestion that the expedition may never have actually left Athens, see Andrewes, op. cit. 4.154.
73 Thuc. 5.82.5–6.
74 Plut. *Alc*. 15.4–5.
75 Andrewes (op. cit. 5.261–4) also stresses the importance of the re-emergence of the Argive democrats on Alcibiades' popularity.
76 Thuc. 5.83.1–2.

77 The Athenians had first attempted to add Melos to their empire in 426 (Thuc. 3.91.1–3).
78 Thuc. 5.85–113.
79 Xen. *Hell*. 2.2.3.
80 Isoc. 12.63.
81 The complex problem of the interrelationship of these two works is insightfully discussed by A.R. Burn [*CQ* n.s 4 (1954) 138–42), who concludes that they used a common source. This seems to be the best solution to the problem. See also R.J. Littman, *TAPA* 101 (1970) 266, n.6.
82 Plut. *Alc*. 16.5–6; [Andoc.] 4.22–3.
83 Thuc. 3.91.
84 *Schol*. on Aristoph. *Av*. 186; *HCT* 4.190.
85 Thuc. 5.84.1.
86 So Kagan, *Peace of Nicias* 153.
87 *IG* I$^3$ 71 = *ML* 69.
88 For Plataea, see Thuc. 3.68; for Hysia, Thuc. 5.83.1–2; for Scione, Thuc. 5.32.1.
89 [Andoc.] 4.22–3. Plutarch (*Alc*. 16.5) makes a similar statement. For the relationship of these two sources, see n. 81 above.
90 Raubitschek's attempt [(1948) op. cit.] to prove that the speech is a genuine fifth-century document and that it may have been delivered by Phaeax has found little acceptance.
91 So Littman, op. cit. 266.
92 Thuc. 6.16.2. For the date and for the tradition that Alcibiades' chariot teams came in first, second and third, see Dover, op. cit. 4.246–7.
93 Plut. *Alc*. 11.1–2. Trans. B. Perrin.
94 [Andoc.] 4.30; Plut. *Alc*. 12.1.
95 Thuc. 6.16.1–2.
96 Plut. *Nic*. 3.4–4.1. For the date see F. Courby, *BCH* 45 (1921) 174–241, esp. 184–5. For the comparison between Nicias at Delos and Alcibiades at Olympia, see Kagan, *Peace of Nicias* 153–5.
97 Plut. *Alc*. 12.3. For slightly different versions of this story, see Diod. 13.74.3 and [Andoc.] 4.26.
98 Davies, *APF* 502; R. Münsterberg, *Festschrift Theodor Gomperz* (Vienna 1979) 299.
99 Hatzfeld 140.

## Chapter four  Sicily and defection

1 For the names of Themistocles' daughters, see Plut. *Them*. 32.2. For his interest in the west, see e.g. Hdt. 8.62.
2 The date of this alliance (*IG* I$^3$ 11 = *ML* 37) is controversial. Only the last two letters (*-ov*) of the archon's name can be read clearly. Many earlier historians (e.g. Hatzfeld 142–3) chose Ariston, archon in 454/453, because Diodorus (11.86.2) mentioned a war between

Segesta and a neighbouring city at that time. A.E. Raubitschek's
suggestion [*TAPA* 75 (1944) 10, n. 3] of Habron and the year 458/457
has won impressive support [B.D. Meritt, *BCH* 88 (1964) 413–15;
R. Meiggs and D. Lewis in *ML*, 80–2]. H.B. Mattingly's arguments
[*Historia* 12 (1963) 267–9] for Antiphon and 418/417 are less popular
both because of the letter forms and because of the likelihood that
Thucydides would have mentioned a treaty in that year. Although
Mattingly later expressed reservations about this reading [*Istituto
Italiano di Numismatica, Annali*, suppl. to 12–14 (1965–7) 201–21,
esp. 205, n. 7 and 213], his advocacy of Antiphon has gained support
from J.D. Smart [*JHS* 92 (1972) 128–44] and T.E. Wick [*JHS* 95
(1975) 186–90 and *CP* 76 (1981) 118–21]. Although Habron and
458/457 still have impressive endorsements, the supporters of
Antiphon have cast a considerable amount of doubt on this date.

3 So J. de Romilly, *Thucydides and Athenian Imperialism* (New York
  1979) 201.

4 The Athenian alliances with Rhegion (*IG* I$^3$ 53 = *ML* 63) and
  Leontini (*IG* I$^3$ 54 = *ML* 64) can be dated with certainty to the
  archonship of Apseudes in the year 433/432. However, many
  historians (see *ML* 171–5) think that the prescript was added to an
  earlier decree and that the original treaties date to to the 440s.
  E. Ruschenbusch [*ZPE* 19 (1975) 225–32] has cast considerable
  doubt on this 'established' interpretation. If these alliances should be
  dated to 433/432 and the Segesta alliance to 418/417, it does not
  necessarily mean that Athens had no interest in the west before the
  Peloponnesian War. Her alliance with Corcyra in 433 was doubtless
  motivated, in part, by a desire for westward expansion.

5 Thuc. 3.86, 3.90, 3.103, 3.115, 4.1–2, 4.24–5.

6 Thucydides (3.86.4) says that Athens' true aims were to prevent the
  shipment of grain to Sparta from the west and to explore the
  possibility of taking control of Sicily. There can be little doubt that
  the Athenians intended to exploit the problems in Sicily for their own
  self- interest. However, it seems unlikely that they had any such
  clear-cut ideas in mind or that these aims were actually voted on by
  the assembly. The Athenians were, at the time that they sent the
  expedition, committed to the siege of Mytilene and to too many other
  enterprises to contemplate seriously the conquest of Sicily.

7 Thuc. 4.59–64.

8 Thuc. 5.4–5.

9 Aristophanes (*Eq.* 1302–5) associates Hyperbolus with the desire to
  mount an expedition to conquer Carthage. Although this seems to be
  a comic exaggeration, Hyperbolus had probably been a strong
  promoter of a western policy.

10 Thuc. 6.48.

11 Thuc. 6.1.1.

12 Thuc. 6.13.1. Nicias' speech implies that it was primarily the young
   men who wanted an expedition. The older men presumably
   remembered with greater clarity the annual invasions from Sparta

and the horrors of the plague.

13 Diod. 12.83.1–3.

14 Thuc. 6.46.3–5.

15 Thucydides (6.46.3) says 'in their own and neighbouring cities'. K.J. Dover (*HCT* 4.313) points out that there were no neighbouring cities that were likely to co-operate.

16 There is epigraphical evidence (*IG* I$^3$ 93=*ML* 78) to suggest that the Athenians, at first, considered sending only one general. This general presumably would have been Alcibiades, since Nicias probably expressed reluctance to lead a campaign he so strongly opposed (so Kagan, *Peace of Nicias* 169–71).

17 Thuc. 6.8.3–6.26.1. Nicias' first speech is 6.9–14.

18 Thuc. 6.15.

19 Thuc. 2.65.11. H.D. Westlake [*CQ* n.s. 8 (1958) 102–10] concluded that Thucydides had the recall of Alcibiades in mind 'almost exclusively,' but that Thucydides' narrative of the expedition does not justify the idea that Alcibiades' leadership would have led to victory. See pp. 62–5 and n. 79.

20 Thuc. 6.16–18.

21 Thuc. 6.48.

22 See e.g. Thuc. 2.62–4. The tone of these two speeches is similar; the content, of course, is quite different. De Romilly, who compares and contrasts the two speeches, concludes that 'there are indeed connections but no primary and peremptory relation' (op. cit. 210–13).

23 Thuc. 6.19.

24 Thuc. 6.20–5.

25 Thuc. 6.24.4.

26 Plut. *Nic.* 13.9; *Alc.* 17.5.

27 Plut. *Nic.* 13.7–8; *Alc.* 17.5–6.

28 Plut. *Nic.* 13.

29 C.A. Powell [*Historia* 28 (1979) 18] substantiates the incident with a citation from Aristophanes' *Lysistrata* (ll. 387–96).

30 Plut. *Nic.* 13.11; see also Aristoph. *Lys.* 387–97. For the disputed date of the Adonia, see Dover, op. cit. 4.223–4, 271.

31 Thuc. 6.27.1.

32 Ibid.

33 Aristoph. *Lys.* 1094; Dover, op. cit. 4.288–9.

34 Thuc. 6.27.2.

35 Andoc. 1.14, 36.

36 So P. Green [*Armada from Athens* (New York 1970) 116] who believes that 'the commission was designed to represent all major political groupings in Athens'.

37 Thuc. 8.65.2; Plut. *Alc.* 19.1–3.

38 Andoc. 1.11.

39 Thuc. 6.28; Plut. *Alc.* 19.1–3.

40 Few modern historians see any genuine relationship between these two incidents for reasons that will be discussed in the next few

paragraphs. Dover notes that there were some men who were
accused of both crimes and concludes that 'to this extent the
Athenians were right in believing that the same people, or at least the
same section of society, were concerned with both impieties' (op. cit.
4.288). Dover makes no attempt to show any causal relationship
between the two events, and so I assume he means only that both
pranks were perpetrated by aristocrats who had the leisure and
inclination for such foolishness.

41 E.F. Benson [*The Life of Alcibiades* (London 1928) 154–6] and
Hatzfeld (177–81, 191) believe that Alcibiades was innocent of both
charges.

42 Andoc. 1.15–18.

43 Plut. *Alc*. 22.4.

44 So D. MacDowell, *Andokides: On the Mysteries* (Oxford 1962) 192.

45 Dover, op. cit. 4.283.

46 Kagan, *Peace of Nicias*, 204–6.

47 Thuc. 6.28.

48 Plutarch adds the plausible detail that these speakers were opponents
of Alcibiades but that they were not publicly known to be so (*Alc*.
19.5–6).

49 For example, G. Gilbert, *Beiträge zur inneren Geschichte Athens*
(Leipzig 1877) 250; E. Meyer, *Geschichte des Altertums* (Basel 1954)
4.506; B.W. Henderson, *The Great War between Athens and Sparta*
(London 1927) 255–357.

50 Green, op.cit. 123–6.

51 MacDowell, op. cit. 192–193; M.F. McGregor, *Phoenix* 19 (1965)
35–6; Kagan, *Peace of Nicias*, 207–9.

52 Bury-Meiggs 294–6.

53 J.L. Marr, *CQ* n.s. 21 (1971) esp. 337–8.

54 Thuc. 5.45–6.

55 Thuc. 8.6.

56 See A. Andrewes, *HCT* 5.19–20, who concludes that the normal
practice would be to delay the expedition.

57 Grote 6.8.

58 Thuc. 8.65.

59 Andoc. 1.60–8.

60 So MacDowell, op. cit. 190–3, and Kagan, *Peace of Nicias*, 208–9.
Not all hetairiai had oligarchic sympathies, as is sometimes thought.
See Dover's arguments against this in op. cit. 4.286. Andocides,
however, was often labelled an oligarch (see e.g. Plut. *Them*. 32.4
and Plut. *Alc*. 21.2). For a detailed study that agrees essentially with
the works cited above, see Olivier Aurenche, *Les groupes
d'Alcibiade, de Léogoras et de Teucros* (Paris 1974) esp. 89–101, 176.

61 Hatzfeld's attempt (177–81) to prove that Alcibiades was involved in
the Mysteries of the Thracian goddess Kotytto is not convincing and
has won, to my knowledge, no support.

62 Andoc. 1.67; *HCT* 4.286; MacDowell, op. cit. 192.

63 See Grote (6.9, n. 3) 'The fact is, that no foreigners could well have

done the deed: it required great familiarity with all the buildings, highways, and byways of Athens.'

64 Thuc. 6.31.1.
65 Thuc. 6.44.
66 So Grote 6.18.
67 Since Nicias and Lamachus both died in Sicily, it is often deduced that Thucydides learned of these strategies from Alcibiades. See e.g. P.A. Brunt, *REG* 65 (1952) 59–96, esp. 70 and H. Bengtson, *Zu den strategischen Konzeptionen des Alkibiades* (Munich 1979) 13–14. But see also Dover, op. cit. 4.313–14, for other possible sources.
68 See e.g. Grote 6.28–9, Busolt, III.2.1305 (citing Philistus as the source of Plut. *Nic.* 14) and Green, op. cit. 141.
69 Esp. Thuc. 7.42.3.
70 So Bengtson (1979) op. cit. 13.
71 Thuc. 6.15.2.
72 Thuc. 6.90.
73 Plutarch (*Alc.* 17.3) adds Libya.
74 See Grote's comments (6.74–5) on the 'Grand Design', esp., 'that any such vast designs as those which he [Alcibiades] announces were ever really contemplated even by himself and his immediate friends is very improbable; that they were contemplated by the Athenian public, by the armament, or by Nikias, is utterly incredible.'
75 Thucydides may have been in the Peloponnese at the time (see 5.26.5) and so it is possible that he received reliable information on Alcibiades' speech.
76 Thuc. 6.74; Plut. *Alc.* 22.1.
77 Thuc. 3.90.3–4.
78 Thuc. 6.74.
79 Historians stating or suggesting this view include: Hatzfeld 196–200; Westlake, op. cit. 108; H. Bengtson, *Griechische Geschichte*[2] (Munich 1960) 234; Dover, op. cit. 4.242–3; and E.F. Bloedow, *Alcibiades Re-examined, Historia* Einzelschriften Heft 21 (Wiesbaden 1973) 10–15.
80 Plut. *Alc.* 22.4.
81 Thuc. 6.74.
82 Plut. *Alc.* 22.5; Poll. *Onom.* 10.97.
83 Philochorus, *FGrH* 328 F 134. *IG* $I^3$ 421 (= *ML* 79) records the sale of property that belonged to Alcibiades and others including his uncle Axiochus. See W.K. Pritchett's edition of the stelae [*Hesperia* 22 (1953) 240–9, 268–79; 25 (1956) 276–81; and 30 (1961) 23–5].
84 *Schol.* to Aristoph. *Av.* 766.
85 Plut. *Alc.* 22.5. Plut *Alc.* 33.3 could be interpreted to mean that only the priests of Eleusis were commanded to curse Alcibiades. Diodorus (13.69.2) and Nepos (*Alc.* 4.5) specify only the Eumolpidae.
86 Some ancient sources (Isoc. 16.9; Plut. *Alc.* 23.1) say that Alcibiades went from Elis to Argos and from there to Sparta. Thucydides does not mention Argos. Alcibiades had important ties with the Argives and it would be the logical place for him to seek refuge. However,

there had been trouble there recently (Thuc. 6.61.3), and it may be that he was no longer welcome. Dover (op. cit. 4.360) suggests that Elis may have already been in Spartan control and that Alcibiades went immediately to enemy territory, but this is not certain. Nepos (*Alc.* 4.4) says that Alcibiades went from Elis to Thebes, but it is difficult to understand how this would improve his situation either politically or geographically unless he were trying to get to Persia. There is no doubt that Alcibiades intended to defect eventually, because he had already delivered Messana over to the enemy. It seems logical, however, that he would seek out a neutral state in order to work out the terms of his defection, for he clearly did not trust the Spartans. The tradition that Alcibiades went to Argos may be more than the 'apologia' that Dover (op. cit.) says it is, but it is best to remain sceptical since Thucydides is mute and Isocrates is unreliable.

87 Thuc. 1.138.4.
88 Thuc. 6.89–92.
89 Thucydides (6.93) says that the Spartans had already considered marching against Athens, and that the Corinthians and the Syracusans had made the same requests as Alcibiades and had even used the same arguments (6.88). A growing number of historians have suggested that Thucydides exaggerated Alcibiades' influence in these decisions: so Brunt, op. cit. 71–2; Kagan, *Peace of Nicias* 257, and P.J. Rhodes (Durham 1985) 11.
90 Thuc. 6.105 and 7.18.
91 Thuc. 7.27–8.
92 Plut. *Alc.* 23.3–6.
93 Plut. *Alc.* 23.7–9.
94 Xen. *Hell.* 3.3.1–4.
95 R.J. Littman, *Phoenix* 23 (1969) 269–77 believes that Leotychides was born about 425, but his reconstruction is speculative.
96 Historians who accept the story include: Bury–Meiggs 308; W.S. Ferguson, *CAH* 5.314; V. Ehrenberg, *RE* 6A, *s.v.* 'Timaia', cols 1074–5; G. Glotz, *Histoire grecque* 2.717; Hatzfeld 217–19; Brunt op. cit. 73 n. 2, and C.D. Hamilton, *Ktema* 7 (1982) esp. 290–1. Those who reject the incident as unhistorical include: Beloch 2.188; B. Niese, *RE* 1 *s.v.* 'Agis', col. 818; S. Luria, *Klio* 21 (1927) 404–12, and H.D. Westlake, *JHS* 58 (1938) 31–40, esp. 34. Andrewes (op. cit. 5.26), although unconvinced, presents the case against acceptance. Agis, this argument maintains, would have been about sixty years of age at the birth of Leotychides if the latter were born *c.*413. But Plutarch (*Ages.* 1.2–5) describes Agesilaus as having been brought up as a private citizen and not as an heir apparent. If Agis had not had a son before 413, it is argued, Agesilaus would have been brought up as the successor. Hence Leotychides must have been older and not Alcibiades' son. This argument is not convincing. If Agesilaus were born *c.*444, he would have been about seventeen at the time Agis became king in 427. He

may have become heir apparent at that time, but his education would have been largely over. Plutarch's point is that Agesilaus was brought up as a child by the normal Spartan system of education. It is even possible that Agesilaus was originally excluded from the throne because of his lameness, and only later, because of his personality and perhaps the influence of Lysander, was able to overcome what, for a Spartan, must have been an enormous liability. Littman [op. cit. and *TAPA* 101 (1970) esp. 269, 276] thinks that Alcibiades may have been Timaea's lover, but was not Leotychides' father.

97 Thuc. 8.12.2, 8.45.1.
98 Westlake (1938) op. cit. 31–40.
99 Hatzfeld 214 n.1.
100 Lysias, for example, would surely have made something of it at 14.30.
101 Plut. *Alc*. 23.7–9, and 24.3.
102 Plut. *Alc*. 24.3–4.

## Chapter five    Recall, triumph, and death

1 The primary source for this section is Thucydides 8.1–62.
2 Thuc. 8.12.
3 Thuc. 8.14.2.
4 Thucydides records three different treaties. The first (8.18) was concluded soon after the revolt of Miletus. Thucydides says that this alliance was drafted by Tissaphernes and Chalcideus although it is likely that Alcibiades also took part in the negotiations. [See Hatzfeld 222–3, and Donald Kagan, *The Fall of the Athenian Empire* (Ithaca, NY and London 1987) 49–50.] The treaty asserts that all territory held by the Great King of Persia or by any of his forefathers should be Persian. This statement could be interpreted to mean that the Spartans had handed over the Aegean, Thessaly, and Boeotia to the Persians, but 'it is unlikely that either party had more than Asia Minor in mind' [D.M. Lewis, *Sparta and Persia* (Leiden 1977) 90]. A. Andrewes is probably right when he says that this first treaty was no more than 'a working arrangement between the commanders on the spot' (*HCT* 5.143). The second treaty (Thuc. 8.37) was negotiated by Tissaphernes on the Persian side and Astyochus and Therimenes on the Spartan side. Like the first agreement, this treaty provided for a joint war against Athens and excluded a separate peace for either party. This document stipulated that all troops in Persian territory would be paid by the Great King. The third treaty (Thuc. 8.58) is more formal than the other two and is generally believed to be the definitive agreement between the two nations. The Great King's influence was limited to Asia Minor, but the Spartans explicitly consigned to him the Greeks of that region, some of whom had been free of Persian domination since the time of Xerxes. The Spartan sailors were to be

paid by Tissaphernes until the arrival of the Phoenician navy, at which time the Spartans could borrow money to pay their seamen.
5 Thuc. 8.26.
6 Thuc. 8.44.4.
7 Andrewes (op. cit. 5.96–7, 451) believes that Alcibiades did not defect to Tissaphernes until early in 411. Thuc. 8.45 does not follow in chronological order from the previous chapters, and so the exact date is difficult to pinpoint. Thucydides says that Alcibiades withdrew to Tissaphernes after the battle of Miletus (late summer 412), but how long after the battle is not clear. However, if the new ephors, replacing the board that had included Endius, began their term of office in September, then the orders for Alcibiades' death would probably have come shortly after that (Busolt III.2.1437). Andrewes op. cit. 5.95–6) believes that Alcibiades fabricated the death threat, a suggestion made but later abandoned by Lewis (op. cit. 96 and n. 62). Alcibiades was certainly capable of such a ruse, but it seems entirely credible that the Spartans, perhaps under the pressure of Agis, had turned against him and that they would choose to dispose of him in this manner.
8 Thuc. 8.45.2.
9 Plut. *Alc.* 23.4–5. At 24.5 Plutarch uses the word πολύτροπος to describe Alcibiades, the word Homer uses to describe Odysseus.
10 Plut. *Alc.* 24.7.
11 Thuc. 8.45–6.
12 Thucydides (8.47.2) qualifies Alcibiades' role to some extent by adding that some of the leaders at Samos had come up with the same idea on their own.
13 Thucydides (8.63.4) says that the leaders of the coup did not think Alcibiades a suitable person for an oligarchy. I have argued [*UCLA Historical Journal* 6 (1985) 101–11] that his 'natural constituency was among the sailors who favored democracy and the war policy. He would need victories to strengthen his reputation among those Athenians who still doubted his leadership. Alcibiades was in no position to make peace with the Spartans whom he had just deserted and betrayed' (108).
14 So M.F. McGregor, *Phoenix* 19 (1965) 42.
15 McGregor, op. cit. 27.
16 McGregor, op. cit. 38.
17 Thuc. 8.86.4–5.
18 McGregor, op. cit. 43.
19 Thuc. 6.89.5.
20 Thuc. 8.65.2.
21 Ibid.
22 Thuc. 8.86.4–5.
23 Ibid.
24 For the chronology of these months, see Andrewes, op. cit. 5.185–7.
25 Thuc. 8.47–8.

26  For Phrynichus see Lys. 20.11–12; 25.9. For Pisander see Andoc. 1.36.
27  Thuc. 8.48.
28  Ibid.
29  Hatzfeld (235–6) believed that Alcibiades fabricated the entire
    episode of Phrynichus and Astyochus in order to discredit the
    former. H.D. Westlake [*JHS* 76 (1956) 99–104] thinks that
    Phrynichus believed Alcibiades himself to be a major threat to
    Athens and set out to ruin him. To the extent that Phrynichus
    alerted Tissaphernes to the fact that Alcibiades was collaborating
    with the Athenians and did not have Persia's best interests in mind,
    Westlake argues, he was successful. R. Sealey [*Essays in Greek
    Politics* (New York 1967) 111–32] believes that Phrynichus' motives
    were primarily personal and not ideological. I have argued against
    this idea (op. cit. esp. 107–9).
30  Kagan,op. cit. 123.
31  Ibid.
32  Thuc. 8.50–1.
33  Thuc. 8.50.3; 8.83.3.
34  For example Westlake, op. cit. 102.
35  Thuc. 8.39.2; 8.83.3.
36  Thuc. 8.85.1.
37  Westlake, op. cit. 102.
38  Thuc. 8.27.5.
39  For example T. Lenschau, *RE* 20, col. 908, and P.A. Brunt, *REG*
    65 (1952) 76–7.
40  So P.R. Pouncey, *The Necessities of War* (New York 1980) 133.
41  Thuc. 8.90.
42  Lycurg. 'Against Leocrates,' 113–15.
43  *IG* I³ 102 = *ML* 85.
44  My thinking on this episode has been influenced and stimulated by
    the recent discussion of Kagan (op. cit. 122–30)
45  Thucydides' language at 8.48.3–4 seems to include Phrynichus
    among those who were working to establish an oligarchy.
46  Kagan, op. cit. 126.
47  Grote 243. See also citations in n. 39.
48  Westlake (op. cit. 101–2) has shown why Phrynichus could not
    assume that Astyochus would treat the second letter as he did the
    first. Kagan (op. cit. 127–8) has shown some of the reasons why
    Phrynichus might have thought that the second offer to Astyochus
    might succeed.
49  Thuc. 8.27.5.
50  Kagan op. cit. 55–56, 67.
51  Westlake, op. cit. 102.
52  Kagan, op. cit. 128–9.
53  For the question of whether Tissaphernes ever intended to furnish
    aid to the Athenians, see n. 59.
54  Westlake (op. cit.) sees Astyochus as, 'not a man of very high

ability', achieving some of these goals, almost by accident, and because 'he trusted Alkibiades more than he trusted Phrynichos' (102–3). Kagan (op. cit. 128–9) sees Astyochus' actions as forming more of a deliberate plan.

55  Thuc. 8.53.2.
56  Thuc. 8.54.3.
57  Thuc. 8.54.2. Probably one from each tribe. So Andrewes, op. cit. 5.126.
58  Thuc. 8.56.5.
59  Is it possible that Tissaphernes ever seriously considered allying himself with Athens? Most historians, beginning with Thucydides, think not. Two exceptions are Hatzfeld (239) and Lewis (op. cit. 102). The former thinks that the negotiations here were genuine, but that Tissaphernes had to offer the Great King at least as much from Athens as Sparta was likely to offer. Lewis suggests that the Persians would prefer to deal with the Spartans, but that Tissaphernes had to produce a Greek ally from one side or the other.
60  McGregor, op. cit. 43.
61  Grote hints at this view when he says that Pisander's expressed disappointment at Samos 'created among the armament an impression that Alkibiades was really favourable to the democracy' (6.252).
62  Thuc. 8.65–70 and Ar. *AP* 32.1. The length of time between the Colonus assembly and the seizure of power is controversial. See e.g. P.J. Rhodes, *A Commentary on the Aristotelian Athenaion Politeia* (Oxford 1981) 405–6 and A. Andrewes, *PCPS* 22 (1976) 14–25.
63  Thuc. 8.75.
64  Thuc. 8.81.
65  Thuc. 8.82.1–2.
66  Thuc. 8.86.1–7. There are several incidents in the eighth book of Thucydides that seem to repeat earlier episodes. These 'doublets' are usually taken as one sign that Thucydides had not set this book into its final form i.e. that it is an incomplete rough draft.
L. Holzapfel [*Hermes* 28 (1893) 462–4) argued that this second assembly was a doublet for the one at 8.82.1–2. His argument is not convincing and has been effectively answered by J. Steup [*Thukydides* VIII³ (Berlin 1922) 296] and Andrewes (5.287).
67  Thuc. 8.86.5.
68  Plut. *Alc*. 25.4–5. Trans. by I. Scott-Kilvert, *The Rise and Fall of Athens* (Harmondsworth 1960) 271.
69  In an unpublished doctoral dissertation ('Myth of the hoplite oligarchy: Athens 411/10 B.C.', University of California, Los Angeles 1986), Ralph Gallucci argues that there was no government of the Five Thousand and that democracy was restored immediately after the fall of the Four Hundred. Gallucci offers compelling evidence that the hoplite oligarchy of the Five Thousand

and the separation of this government from the democracy-in-exile on Samos after the fall of the Four Hundred are the 'inventions of modern scholarship' (10). When Thucydides (8.97.1) says that they voted to hand over affairs to the Five Thousand, Gallucci maintains, the Athenians were simply returning to the letter of the Cleisthenic constitution, which restricted the magistracies to the two highest property classes. This restriction had long been ignored, and in 457 magistracies had been opened to the zeugitai, but this was not a fundamental change in the constitution. The decision to insist on hoplite status as a prerequisite for office may have been motivated by a desire to recall Alcibiades, who 'might still be able to gain the Persians as allies and their gold' by saying that leadership at Athens was in the hands of the upper classes 'and not the radical democrats' (12). Gallucci's work is based on an idea first discussed by G.E.M. de Ste Croix [*Historia* 5 (1956) 1–23].

70 Plutarch (*Alc*. 33.1) quotes an elegy of Critias in which he (Critias) claims to have sponsored the bill that recalled Alcibiades. Diodorus (13.38.2), following Ephorus, and Nepos (*Alc*. 5.4) both say that it was Theramenes who was primarily responsible for the recall of Alcibiades. These two statements are not contradictory, and it may be that the two men worked together for Alcibiades. A. Andrewes [*JHS* 73 (1953) 3, n. 7] thinks that Critias' decree may date to 408/7 rather than to 411. H. Bengtson [*Zu den strategischen Konzeptionen des Alkibiades* (Munich 1979) 21–4] thinks that Alcibiades was not officially recalled until shortly before he returned to Athens, and he assigns that return to the year 408. No conclusion concerning chronology may be drawn from this passage in Plutarch, but it is possible that Alcibiades was recalled by the Five Thousand in 411 and again by the full democracy at some later date.

71 Thuc. 8.88.

72 Thuc. 8.108.1.

73 Xen. *Hell*. 1.1.4–7 and Diod. 13.45–7. Diodorus' account of the battle of Abydus differs in certain details from Xenophon's, but it corroborates the fact that Alcibiades' intervention on behalf of the Athenians was the decisive factor in their victory.

74 Kagan, op. cit. 235.

75 Thuc. 8.88.

76 .Xen. *Hell*. 1.1.9.

77 Xen. *Hell*. 1.1.10.

78 Xen. *Hell*. 1.1.10; *Diod*. 13.68.2.

79 Plut. *Alc*. 28.2.

80 Xen. *Hell*. 1.1.11–12.

81 Xen. *Hell*. 1.1.11–23; Diod. 13.49.2–13.51.8.

82 Most modern historians have followed Xenophon's account. These include: Busolt III.2.1527; Beloch, 1.394; W.S. Ferguson, *CAH* 5.343; N.G.L. Hammond, *A History of Greece*, 3rd edn (1986) 411, n.1, and Bengtson (op. cit.) 22. Beloch, Ferguson, and Bengtson,

while preferring Xenophon, allow some details from Diodorus. The
few historians who prefer Diodorus' account include Grote
(6.344–5); Hatzfeld (271), and R.J. Littman, [*TAPA* 99 (1968)
265–72. Littman has shown conclusively, to my mind, that
Xenophon's account is inferior since it is based on the absurdity
that Mindarus would hold naval 'maneuvers some distance from the
harbor during a heavy rain' (268). Littman's preference for
Diodorus has also been endorsed by A. Andrewes [*JHS* 102 (1982)
15–25] and Kagan (op. cit. 236–46).

83  Our two major sources disagree on the number of ships. Xenophon
    says that the Athenians had eighty-six ships, and the
    Peloponnesians sixty. Diodorus says that the Peloponnesians had
    eighty ships and were numerically superior to the Athenians.
    Diodorus' numbers are frequently wrong [see R. Meiggs, *The
    Athenian Empire* (Oxford 1972) 447–52], but there is no easy way
    to reconcile this discrepancy. The length and intensity of the battle
    suggest that the two sides were evenly matched.

84  Xen. *Hell*. 1.1.14.

85  Diodorus (13.50.2) says twenty. Plutarch's forty (*Alc*. 28.6) is a
    better choice, because it 'is unlikely that Mindarus would be
    deceived by so small a fleet' [Littman, op. cit. 269, n. 6). Plutarch's
    account of the battle (*Alc*. 28.2–10) borrows elements from both
    Xenophon and Diodorus, or more likely from Ephorus, Diodorus'
    source. His account utilizes Xenophon's rainstorm, but also
    includes Alcibiades' strategy of drawing out Mindarus, as described
    by Diodorus.

86  So Andrewes (1982) op. cit. 21.

87  So Kagan, op. cit. 242.

88  So Andrewes (1982) op. cit. 22.

89  Diod. 13.51.6.

90  So Littman, op. cit. 268.

91  Xen. *Hell*. 1.1.23.

92  Diod. 13.52–3.

93  Ibid.

94  So Ferguson, op. cit. 5.344.

95  This biography follows the chronology developed by Ferguson (op.
    cit. 5.483–485) for the years 410–406. This chronology is accepted
    by the majority of historians today. However, some [notably
    H. Bengtson, op. cit. 23–28; *Griechische Geschichte*[2] (Munich
    1960) 238; and *Griechische Staatsmänner* (Munich 1983) 175–7] still
    follow the chronology adopted by Busolt (III.2.1529–32), which
    places the battles of Chalcedon and Byzantium in 409, Alcibiades'
    return to Athens in 408, and the battle of Notium in 407.

96  Xen. *Hell*. 1.1.35–6. Thucydides (8.8.2) says that Clearchus was
    given the command of an expedition to the Hellespont in the
    summer of 412. The expedition did not actually leave until the
    following summer (Thuc. 8.80). The sources do not report that
    Clearchus returned home after that time, but I agree with

Andrewes (*HCT* 5.21) that this is the most likely explanation.
97 It is possible that Alcibiades was removed from his generalship in
the year 410/9 by the restored democracy [so Andrewes (1953) op.
cit. 3]. C.W. Fornara [*The Athenian Board of Generals from 501 to
404, Historia* Einzelschriften Heft 16 (Wiesbaden 1971) 68–9] does
not believe that new elections were held, but concedes that 'his
position was very likely not "official"' for this year as well as for
409/8. It is difficult to believe that Alcibiades lost his influence with
the fleet, no matter what his official position might have been. He
had been elected general by the fleet in 411 without the city's
permission, and he probably remained in control now, after his
victory at Cyzicus.
98 Diod. 13.64.5–7.
99 Xen. *Hell.* 1.2.1–13.
100 Xen. *Hell.* 1.2.13–17.
101 Andrewes [(1953) op. cit. 2–9] sees an ideological conflict here
between the democrat Thrasyllus and the moderate Alcibiades, but
this is, perhaps, overly schematic.
102 Xen. *Hell.* 1.2.16.
103 Xen. *Hell.* 1.3.2–4.
104 Xen. *Hell.* 1.3.4.
105 Xen. *Hell.* 1.1.23.
106 Alcibiades was presumably fighting Pharnabazus, but Xenophon's
account (*Hell.* 1.3.5–7) does not make this point clear. The events
are: (a) Pharnabazus approaches the wall, (b) Thrasyllus fights
Hippocrates, (c) Alcibiades comes to the rescue, (d) Hippocrates is
killed, and his men flee, and (e) Pharnabazus retires. Diodorus'
briefer account (13.66.1–2) does not mention Pharnabazus but
simply pits Alcibiades against Hippocrates. Plutarch (*Alc.* 30.1) has
Alcibiades fight Hippocrates and Pharnabazus simultaneously and
defeat them both.
107 Plutarch (*Alc.* 30.3–10) wrote an elaborate description of this
operation which he probably took from Ephorus since it agrees with
the briefer account in Diodorus (13.66.4). The details of this
account should be read with scepticism.
108 *IG* I³ 118 = *ML* 87. In this treaty Alcibiades agreed not to seek
lost property except land and houses. He promised a restoration of
hostages and guaranteed Selymbrian autonomy.
109 At this point Ephorus' version (Diod. 13.67.1–6 and Plut. *Alc.*
31.3–5) diverges from the account of Xenophon (*Hell.* 1.3.14–22),
which is preferred here. Ephorus portrays the Athenians as
deceiving the Byzantines with an ingenious device. Alcibiades
pretended to leave for Ionia with the fleet and the infantry. That
night the fleet returned and began to drag off the enemy ships with
as loud a noise as they could muster. The garrison and those
Byzantines who were not aware of the plot hurried to the harbour
to fight for their ships. While the Peloponnesians and their allies
were outside the walls, Alcibiades and his infantry took possession

of the city. The main reason for rejecting this addition of Ephorus is that it seems unnecessary. Xenophon's account is logical and certainly more economical. Life, however, is not always logical. The device that Diodorus and Plutarch record is consistent with the type of strategy Alcibiades was known to employ, and we cannot reject this incident with absolute certainty.

110 Xen. *Hell*. 1.4.11–12; see also Kagan, op. cit. 287–9.
111 Xen. *Hell*. 1.4.18.
112 Xen. *Hell*. 1.4.12; Plut. *Alc*. 34.1–2.
113 Xen. *Hell*. 1.4.20.
114 See p. 121, n. 83.
115 Diod. 13.69.2.
116 For which priests were involved, see p. 121 n. 85.
117 Or *hegemon autokrator*. Xenophon (*Hell*. 1.4.20), Diodorus (13.69.3), and Plutarch (*Alc*. 33.2) all use similar language. The ten Athenian generals are usually thought to be colleagues, elected without any hierarchy or speciality, but there were certain irregularities in the last years of the war. See Fornara, op. cit. 11–19, 79–80.
118 The fullest account is in Plut. *Alc*. 34.4–7.
119 Xen. *Hell*. 1.5.6–7.
120 Xen. *Hell*. 1.4.21–2.
121 Xenophon (*Hell*. 1.5.8–9) says only that the Athenians sent ambassadors to Cyrus through Tissaphernes. Grote (6.375) suggests that this embassy was Alcibiades' idea.
122 Busolt (III.2.1574–6) believed that Alcibiades deliberately planned to leave Lysander under guard while he went on to reconquer northern Ionia. Lysander would be forced to either fight or stand by helplessly while Alcibiades was free to manoeuvre without Spartan interference. This is an attractive idea, but there is no evidence for it. M. Amit [*Grazer Beiträge* 3 (1975) 1–13] has a similar idea. He believes that Alcibiades and Thrasybulus had begun an ambitious programme of reconquest and that Antiochus was an integral part of that programme. Since the generals did not achieve any success and since Antiochus perished and so was unable to deny the charges, Alcibiades and the other generals conspired to withhold information on the failed campaign and put the blame for Notium on Antiochus, claiming that he exceeded his orders. Again, this is an interesting idea, but there is no evidence in the sources to support it.
123 Xen. *Hell*. 1.5.11.
124 Plut. *Lys*. 5.1.
125 Plut. *Alc*. 35.5.
126 Nep. *Alc*. 7.1–2.
127 Diod. 13.71.1; 13.73.3–5.
128 So Kagan, op. cit. 308–9 and n. 65, 314–15.
129 Kagan, op. cit. 315.
130 This account of the battle of Notium is based on *Hell. Oxy*. 4.1–4

(Teubner ed.); Xen. *Hell*. 1.5.12–14; Diod. 13.71.2–4, and Plut. *Alc*. 35.6–8 and *Lys*. 5.1–3.

131  D. Lotze [*Lysander und der peloponnesische Krieg* (Berlin 1964) 20–2] implies that Antiochus was trying to use the kind of strategy that Alcibiades had applied at Cyzicus.

132  *Hell. Oxy*. 4.2.

133  This scenario was implied by Maas in an appendix to an article by F. Jacoby [*CQ* 44 (1950) 8–11] and endorsed by Andrewes [(1982) op. cit. esp. pp. 17–19]. I.A.F. Bruce [*An Historical Commentary on the Hellenica Oxyrhynchia* (Cambridge 1967) 36] finds the idea attractive but rejects it in the belief that the two traditions cannot be reconciled.

134  Xen. *Hell*. 1.5.14; Diod. 13.71.4.

135  Plut. *Alc*. 36.1; Diod. 13.73.6.

136  See p. 91 concerning the incident at Cyme.

137  Diod. 13.73.6.

138  Plut. *Alc*. 36.2.

139  Xen. *Hell*. 1.5.16.

140  Xen. *Hell*. 1.5.18; Diod. 13.74.1.

141  Only six of the generals came to Athens to face charges (Xen. *Hell*. 1.7.1–2).

142  Nep. *Alc*. 7.4.

143  Diod. 13.74.2.

144  Plut. *Alc*. 36.3.

145  Nep. *Alc*. 7.4–5.

146  Aristophanes' *Frogs* (1420–34), produced in 405, shows that Athens was still interested in Alcibiades. There is a contest in this comedy between the spirits of Euripides and Aeschylus, and both are required to comment on what the city should do about Alcibiades.

147  The story of Alcibiades' visit to the Athenians forms an essential element of the narrative of the battle of Aegospotami. Historians, until recently, have usually preferred Xenophon's account (*Hell*. 2.1. 20–32). As with the battles of Cyzicus and Notium, however, there is a growing trend to prefer Diodorus' (13.105.1–106.7). Recent historians of this opinion include: C. Ehrhardt [*Phoenix* 24 (1970) 225–8], B.S. Strauss [*AJP* 104 (1983) 24–35] and Kagan (op. cit. 386–93). I have taken certain details from Xenophon, but generally follow Diodorus. There is no reason not to accept both Alcibiades' offer of help (Diod. 13.105.3–4) and his advice to the Athenians (Xen. *Hell*. 2.1.25–6). Of the other accounts of the battle, Plutarch (*Alc*. 36.6–37.5; *Lys*. 10–11) derives mainly from Xenophon, while Nepos (*Alc*. 8) generally follows Diodorus.

148  Diodorus' version differs in many details from Xenophon's (*Hell*. 2.1.27–8, but it agrees with it to the extent that Lysander took the Athenians by surprise and captured most of their triremes.

149  The numbers come from Diod. 13.105.1 and 13.106.1.

150  So Lotze, op. cit. 34.

151  So Ehrhardt, op. cit. 227 and Kagan, op. cit. 391–3.

152 Nep. *Alc*. 9.1–2.
153 Nep. *Alc*. 9.3.
154 This date is uncertain. See Lewis, op. cit. 120 and n. 81.
155 Diod. 14.11.2 (citing Ephorus); Nep. *Alc*. 9.5. P.J. Rhodes
    [(Durham 1985) 17–18] doubts this detail but does not elaborate.
    Cyrus had already been accused of treason at the time of Darius'
    funeral (Xen. *Anab*. 1.3), but he had been released. As soon as he
    returned to the west he began to gather Greek troops in secret
    (Xen. *Anab*. 1.4–6). So it is not impossible that Alcibiades had
    information that would have been valuable to Artaxerxes. Neither
    does it seem unlikely that Alcibiades would seek an audience with
    the Great King. As events were soon to prove, Alcibiades could not
    rely on Pharnabazus' hospitality.
156 Diod. 14.11.1–4; Nep. *Alc*. 10; Justin 5.8; Plut. *Alc*. 38.5–39.9.
157 Paus. 2.2.5.
158 Thuc. 6.62.3–4.
159 Plut. *Nic*. 15.4.
160 Nep. *Alc*. 1.1.

# Select bibliography

Amit, M. (1975) 'La Campagne d'Ionie de 407/6 et la bataille de Notion', *Grazer Beiträge* 3: 1–13.

Anderson, J.K. (1954) 'A topographical and historical study of Achaea', *BSA* 49: 72–92.

Andrewes, A. (1953) 'The generals in the Hellespont, 410–407 B.C.', *JHS* 73 2–9.

(1982) 'Notion and Kyzikos: the sources compared', *JHS* 102: 15–25.

Aurenche, O. (1974) *Les groupes d'Alcibiade, de Léogoras et de Teucros*, Paris.

Barber, G.L. (1935) *The Historian Ephorus*, Cambridge.

Beloch, K.J. (1884) *Die attische Politik seit Perikles*, Leipzig.

Bengtson, H. (1960) *Griechische Geschichte*[2], Munich.

(1979) *Zu den strategischen Konzeptionen des Alkibiades*, Munich.

(1983) *Griechische Staatsmänner*, Munich.

Benson, E.F. (1928) *The Life of Alcibiades*, London.

Bicknell, P. (1975) 'Alkibiades and Kleinias: a study in Athenian Genealogy', *MPhL* 1: 51–64.

Bloedow, E.F. (1973) *Alcibiades Reexamined, Historia* Einzelschriften Heft 21, Wiesbaden.

Bourriot, F. (1976) *Recherches sur la nature du génos*, Lille.

Bowra, C.M. (1971) *Periclean Athens*, New York.

Bruce, I.A.F. (1967) *An Historical Commentary on the Hellenica Oxyrhynchia*, Cambridge.

Brunt, P.A. (1952) 'Thucydides and Alcibiades', *REG* 65: 59–96.

Burn, A.R. (1954) 'A biographical source of Phaiax and Alkibiades?', *CQ* n.s. 4: 138–42.

Cawkwell, G. (1979) 'Introduction', *A History of My Times*, Harmondsworth.

Connor, W.R. (1971) *The New Politicians of Fifth-Century Athens*, Princeton, NJ.

Courby, F. (1921) 'Le sanctuaire d'Apollon Délien', *BCH* 45:174–241.

Davies, J.K. (1983) *Democracy and Classical Greece*, Stanford, Cal.

Delebecque, E. (1965) *Thucydide et Alcibiade*, Aix-en-Provence.

Dittenberger, W. (1902) 'Die Familie des Alkibiades', *Hermes* 37: 1–8.

Dover, K.J. (1968) *Lysias and the Corpus Lysiacum*, Berkeley and Los Angeles.

(1978) *Greek Homosexuality*, Cambridge, Mass.

Dover, K.J. (ed.) (1980) *Plato: Symposium*, Cambridge.

Edmonds, J. (1957) *The Fragments of Attic Comedy*, Leiden.

Ehrhardt, C. (1970) 'Xenophon and Diodorus on Aegospotami', *Phoenix* 24: 225–8.

Ellis W.M. (1980) 'Alcibiades and the Battle of Cyzicus'. *UCLA Historical Journal* 1.

(1985) 'Reasons for the coup of the Four Hundred', *UCLA Historical Journal* 6.

Ferguson, W.S. (1938) 'The Salaminioi of Heptaphylai and Sounion', *Hesperia* 7: 1–74.

Finley, J.H. (1942) *Thucydides*, Cambridge, Mass.

Finley, M.I. (1962) 'Athenian demagogues', *Past and Present* 21: 3–24.

(1985) *Democracy Ancient and Modern*, London.

Fornara, C.W. (1971) *The Athenian Board of Generals from 501 to 404*, *Historia* Einzelschriften Heft 16, Wiesbaden.

Forrest, W.G. (1956) 'The First Sacred War', *BCH* 80: 33–52.

Fuqua, C. (1965) 'Possible implications of the ostracism of Hyperbolus', *TAPA* 96: 165–79.

Gagarin, M. (1977) 'Socrates' *Hybris* and Alcibiades' failure', *Phoenix* 31: 22–37.

Gilbert, G. (1877) *Beiträge zur inneren Geschichte Athens*, Leipzig.

Glotz, G. (1925–36) *Histoire grecque*, Paris.

Gomme, A.W. (1933) *The Population of Athens*, Oxford.

(1962) *More Essays in Greek History and Literature*, Oxford.

Green, P. (1970) *Armada from Athens*, New York.

Grenfell, B.D. and Hunt, A.S. (eds) (1903) *The Oxyrhynchus Papyri*, III, London.

Grote, G. (1888) *A History of Greece*, London.

Hamilton, C.D. (1982) 'Étude chronologique sur le règne d'Agésilas', *Ktema* 7: 281–96.

Hammond, N.G.L. (1986) *A History of Greece*, 3rd edn, Oxford.

Hansen, M.H. (1982) 'Demographic reflections on the number of Athenian citizens', *AJAH* 7: 172–89.

Harrison, A.R.W. (1968) *The law of Athens: the family and property*, Oxford.

Henderson, B.W. (1927) *The Great War between Athens and Sparta*, London.

Hertzberg, G.F. (1853) *Alkibiades der Staatsmann und Feldherr*, Halle.

Jacoby, F. (1949) *Atthis*, Oxford.

Kaerst, J. (ed.) (1911) *Die Chronik des Eusebios*, Leipzig.

Kagan, D. (1969) *The Outbreak of the Peloponnesian War*, Ithaca, NY and London.

(1974) *The Archidamian War*, Ithaca, NY, and London.

(1981) *The Peace of Nicias and the Sicilian Expedition*, Ithaca, NY and London.

(1987) *The Fall of the Athenian Empire*, Ithaca, NY and London.

Kahn, C.H. (1981) 'Did Plato write Socratic dialogues', *CQ* n.s.31: 305–20.

Kebric, R.B. (1976) 'Implications of Alcibiades' relationship with Endius', *Mnemosyne* 29: 72–8.

Kolbe, W. (1930) *Thukydides im Lichte der Urkunden*, Stuttgart.

Lang, M.L. (1972) 'Cleon as the anti-Pericles', *CP* 67: 159–169.

Lazenby, J.F. (1985) *The Spartan Army*, Warminster.

Lesky, A. (1966) *A History of Greek Literature*, London.

Lewis, D.M. (1977) *Sparta and Persia*, Leiden.

Liebeschuetz, W. (1968) 'Thucydides and the Sicilian expedition', *Historia* 17: 289–306.

Littman, R.J. (1968) 'The strategy of the battle of Cyzicus', *TAPA* 99: 265–72.

(1969) 'A new date for Leotychidas', *Phoenix* 23: 269–77.

(1970) 'The loves of Alcibiades', *TAPA* 101: 263–276.

Lossau, M. (1969) 'ΔHMAΓΩΓOΣ, Fehlen und Gebrauch bei Aristophanes und Thukydides', *Politeia und Res Publica . . . dem Andenken R. Starks gewidmet*, Wiesbaden: 174–241.

Lotze, D. (1964) *Lysander und der peloponnesische Krieg*, Berlin.

Luria, S. (1927) 'Zum politischen Kampf in Sparta gegen Ende des 5. Jahrhunderts', *Klio* 21: 404–12.

MacDowell, D. (1962) *Andokides: on the Mysteries*, Oxford.

McGregor, M.F. (1941) 'Cleisthenes of Sicyon and the Panhellenic Festivals', *TAPA* 72: 266–87.

(1965) 'The genius of Alkibiades', *Phoenix* 19: 27–46.

Marr, J.L. (1971) 'Andocides' part in the Mysteries and Hermae affairs, 415 B.C.', *CQ* n.s. 21: 326–38.

Mattingly H.B. (1961) 'The Athenian Coinage Decree', *Historia* 10; 148–88.

(1963) 'The growth of Athenian imperialism', *Historia* 12: 257–73.

(1965–7) 'Athens and the western Greeks', *Istituto Italiano di Numismatica, Annali* suppl. to 12–14: 201–21.

(1970) '"Epigraphically the Twenties are too Late"', *BSA* 65: 129–33.

Meiggs, R. (1972) *The Athenian Empire*, Oxford.

Meyer, E. (1954) *Geschichte des Altertums*[5], Basel.

Meritt, B.D. (1939) 'Greek inscriptions', *Hesperia* 8: 48–82.

(1964) 'The alliance between Athens and Egesta', *BCH* 88: 413–15.

Münsterberg, R. (1979) 'Zum Rennstallprocess des Alkibiades', *Festschrift Theodor Gomprez*, Vienna.

Perrin, B. (1912) *Plutarch's Nicias and Alcibiades*, New York.

Plutarch, (1960) *The Rise and Fall of Athens*, trans. Ian Scott-Kilvert, Harmondsworth.

Pouncey, P.R. (1980) *The Necessities of War*, New York.

Powell, C.A. (1979) 'Religion and the Sicilian expedition', *Historia* 28: 15–31.

Pusey, N.M. (1940) 'Alcibiades and τὸ φιλόπολι', *Harvard Studies in Classical Philology* 51: 215–30.

Select bibliography

Raubitschek, A.E. (1944) 'Athens and Halikyai', *TAPA* 75: 10–14.
  (1948) 'The case against Alcibiades (Andocides IV)', *TAPA* 79: 191–210.
  (1955) 'Theopompos on Hyperbolus', *Phoenix* 9: 122–6.
  (1955) 'Zur attischen Genealogie', *RhM* 98: 258–62.
Rhodes, P.J. (1981) *A Commentary on the Aristotelian Athenaion Politeia*, Oxford.
  (1985) 'What Alcibiades did or what happened to him', Durham.
Romilly, J. de. (1979) *Thucydides and Athenian Imperialism*, New York.
Ruschenbusch, E. (1975) 'Die Vertrage Athens mit Leontinoi und Rhegion vom Jahre 433/2 v. Chr.', *ZPE* 19: 225–32.
Russell, D.A. (1966) 'Plutarch, "Alcibiades" 1–16', *PCPS* 12: 37–47.
  (1973) *Plutarch*, London.
Scott-Kilvert, I., trans. (1960) *Plutarch: The Rise and Fall of Athens*, Harmondsworth, 222, 255, and 271.
Ste Croix, G.E.M. de (1956) 'The constitution of the five thousand', *Historia*, 5, 1–23.
  (1972) *The Origins of the Peloponnesian War*, London.
  (1981) *The Class Struggle in the Ancient Greek World*, Ithaca.
Schein, S.L. (1974) 'Alcibiades and the politics of misguided love in Plato's *Symposium*', *Theta-Pi* 3: 158–67.
Sealey, R. (1956) 'The entry of Pericles into history', *Hermes* 84: 234–47.
  (1967) *Essays in Greek Politics*, New York.
  (1976) *A History of the Greek City States*, Berkeley and Los Angeles.
Smart, J.D. (1972) 'Athens and Egesta', *JHS* 92: 128–46.
Strauss, B.S. (1983) 'Aegospotami reexamined', *AJP* 104: 24–35.
Taylor, A.E. (1951) *Socrates*, London.
Thompson, W.E. (1968) 'The Chronology of 432/1', *Hermes* 96: 216–32.
Thucydides (1972) *The Peloponnesian War*, trans. Rex Warner, Harmondsworth.
Toepffer, J. (1887) 'ΕΥΠΑΤΡΙΔΑΙ', *Hermes* 22: 479–83.
  (1889) *Attische Genealogie*, Berlin.
Vanderpool, E. (1952) 'The ostracism of the elder Alkibiades', *Hesperia* 21: 1–8.
Westlake, H.D. (1938) 'Alcibiades, Agis and Spartan policy', *JHS* 58: 31–40.
  (1956) 'Phrynichos and Astyochus', *JHS* 76: 99–104.
  (1958) 'Thucydides 2.65.11.', *CQ* n.s. 8: 102–10.
  (1968) *Individuals in Thucydides*, Cambridge.
Wick, T.E. (1976) 'Athens' alliance with Rhegium and Leontini', *Historia* 25: 288–304.
  (1978) 'A note on the date of the Athenian–Egestan alliance', *JHS* 95: 186–90.
  (1981) 'The date of the Athenian–Egestan alliance', *CP* 76: 118–21.
Wilamowitz-Moellendorff, U.v. (1887) 'Demotika Der Attischen Metoeken', *Hermes* 22:107–28.
Woodhead, A.G. (1949) '*IG* I$^2$, 95 and the ostracism of Hyperbolus',

*Hesperia* 18: 78–83.
Woodhouse, W.J. (1933) *King Agis of Sparta*, Oxford.

# Index

Abydus 19–20, 82–3, 84
Aegospotami, battle of 94–5
Aeschines the Socratic 19
Alcibiades: anecdotes about 17–
    20, 30–4; and Archidamian war
    27–30; and battle of Cyzicus
    83–6; character of xiv–xx, 97–8;
    and commission to reassess
    tribute 15, 30–1; coup of the
    Four Hundred 72–80; and
    demagogues 15–17; family 1–9;
    final days 93–7; and 'Grand
    Design' 63, 66; Hellespontine
    war 82–6; marriage 32–4;
    murder 95–7; mutilation of
    herms and profanation of
    Mysteries 58–62; and Olympic
    Festival 50–2; Peloponnesian
    policy 40–5; Potidaean campaign
    24–7; recall to Athenian service
    80–2; return to Athens in 407
    BC 88–90; Sicilian expedition
    54–8, 62–5; and Socrates 20–3;
    in Sparta 65–8; strategy in Sicily
    41, 63–4; youth 9
Alcibiades I (great-great-
    grandfather of Alcibiades) 8
Alcibiades II (grandfather of
    Alcibiades) 6–8, 17
Alcibiades IV (ALcibiades' son) 6,
    34, 51
Alcmaeon 3–4
Alcmaeonids 1–5, 100–1
Alyattes 4
Agariste I 4

Agariste II 5
Agatharchus 31–2
Agesilaus 67
Agis 42–5, 66–8, 69, 88–90, 95
Amphipolis 39; battle of 35
Andocides xviii, 60–1, 102;
    Pseudo-Andocides 7, 33, 49–52
Androcles 16, 48, 61–2, 72–4, 86
Andromachus 59
Antiochus 31, 91–3
Antiphon 17, 80–1;
    Pseudo-Antiphon 17–18, 19–20
Antisthenes 22
Anytus 18–19
Archestratus 25–7
Archidamian war 24, 27–30, 34–5,
    53, 66
Archidamus 28
Areopagus 12
Arginusae, battle of 93
Argive (or Quadruple) Alliance
    15, 37–45, 98
Argos 28, 36–45, 121n86
Ariphron 17–18
Aristotle 3, 12, 15, 100
Artaxerxes II 95–6, 98
Artemisium, battle of 6–8
Astyochus 75–8, 82
Athena Polias 89
Athenaeus xviii, 19–20
Athens: in Archidamian war
    24–35; Argive Alliance 37–40;
    and battle of Mantinea 44–5;
    and demagogues 15–17; and
    Hellespontine war 82–8; and

oligarchic coup of the Four
Hundred 72–80; in Periclean age
9–15; and revolt of allies 69–72;
and Sicilian expedition 54–8,
62–4, 69; western policy 53–4
Axiochus 8–9, 20

Boeotia 9, 30, 88
Bosporus 86–7, 88
Brasidas 35, 90
Byzantium 86, 88, 98

Callias (son of Calliades) 25
Callias II 32
Callias III 33–4
Catana 53, 57, 64
Chaereas 84–5
Chalcedon 86, 87, 88, 98
Chalcideus 69–70
Chalcidice 67
Charicles 58
Chios 69–70
Cimon 7, 9–10, 97
Clazomenae 70, 83, 84, 91
Clearchus 85, 86, 88
Cleinias I (Alcibiades'
great-grandfather) 6–8
Cleinias II (Alcibiades' father) 5–9
Cleinias III 8
Cleinias IV 17
Cleisthenes 3–5, 8, 11
Cleomenes 3, 5
Cleon 16, 31, 35, 37, 62, 86
Cleophon 16, 86
Coeratadas 88
Conon 91, 93, 94
Corcyra 10, 24, 27, 62
Corinth xx, 24–5, 28, 41–3, 44,
60–1, 65–6
Coronea, battle of 5, 6, 8, 9
Cos 82
Croesus 3–4
Cylon 2–3
Cyme 91
Cynossema, battle of 82
Cyrus 90, 95–6
Cyzicus, battle of xvii, 84–6, 87,
88, 92, 98

Daedalus 101
Damon 18
Darius II 70, 78, 88, 90, 95
Decelea 34, 66–7, 88, 89
Delium, battle of 24, 29–30
Democrates 17–18
Demosthenes (general) 29–30
Demosthenes (orator) xvii, 16
Diocleides 61
Diodorus xvi–xvii, 85, 86, 91,
92–3, 95–6, 127n82, 128n83,
131n147
Diognetus 58
Diomedes 51–2
Dorieus 82

Eleusinian Mysteries 58–62, 64,
75, 78, 89–90
Elis 36, 37, 41
Endius 37–40, 69, 86
Ephesus 87, 90, 91, 92
Ephialtes 10
Ephorus xvi–xvii, 51, 92, 95,
129n109
Epimenides of Crete 3
Erythrae 70
Euboea 69
Eumolpidae 90, 121n85
Eupatridae 5–6, 99–102
Euripides 1, 9
Eurymedon 53–4
Eurysaces 101

Five Thousand, the 80–2, 126n69
Four Hundred, the 73–81

Gylippus 66

Helixus 88
*Hellenica Oxyrhynchia* xvii, 92–3
Hellespont 69, 84, 87, 94
Hellespontine war 82–8
Herodotus 3–5, 8
Hipparete 32–4
Hippocrates 85–6, 87
Hipponicus 32–3
Hyccara (Sicily) 97

# Index

Hyperbolus 16, 37, 45–9, 54, 62, 79, 86

Ionia 68, 69–70, 74, 81, 87
Isocrates xviii, 5, 7, 8, 25–6, 51–2, 100–1, 105n43

Kerykes 90, 102

Laches 30, 44
Lais 97
Lamachus 55, 63
Leontini 53–4, 118n4
Lesbos 69
Leotychides 67, 122n96
Lycurgus (orator) xviii
Lysander 90–7
Lysias xviii, 6–7, 34, 112n65; Pseudo-Lysias 20

Macedonia 25–6, 48, 67, 84
Magnesia 75–6, 77
Mantinea 36, 37, 40, 41; battle of 43–5, 65
Megacles I 1–3
Megacles II 4–5
Megacles III 5
Megacles IV 5
Megarian Decree 10, 27
Messana 53, 63, 64
Meton 57–8
Miletus 70
Mindarus 82, 84–6
Myron of Phlya 2

Naxos (Sicily) 53, 57
Nepos xviii, 9, 96–7
Nestor 1
Nicias 17, 33, 34–5, 36–9, 43–5, 45–8, 49–50, 51, 58, 60–1, 72, 97; and debate on Sicilian expedition 54–7; strategy in Sicily 62–3
Notium 90–3

Pactye, Alcibiades' castle at 93–4
Panactum 36, 39
Paphlagonia 96

Perdiccas 25, 48
Pericles xiv, xv, xix, 1, 3, 8, 16, 17–18, 33, 39, 53, 89, 105n55, 110n18 and n19; policy in Peloponnesian war 28; politics in the age of 9–15
Persia: and Alcibiades 71–2, 95–8; and Athens 74–9; and Sparta 65, 69–72, 82–3, 90, 123n4
Phaeax 37, 46, 48, 54
Pharnabazus 69, 82, 83, 87–8, 95–7
Pherecles of Themacus 59
Phidias 1, 9
Philocles 94–5
Phoenician fleet 72, 80, 82
Phormio 25–6
Phrygia 96–7
Phrynichus 70, 74–80, 81
Piraeus 62, 89
Pisander 58, 73–4, 78–80
Pisistratus 4–5
Plato xviii, 1, 17; I Alcibiades xviii, 20, 101–2, 110n2; Charmides 21, 26–7; Crito 22–3; Gorgias xiv, xviii; Laches 30; Phaedo 23; Protagoras xviii, 20; Symposium xviii, 21, 22, 25–7, 109n140; Timaeus 22
Plutarch xiv–xv, xvii–xviii, 6, 47, 51, 67, 85; Alcibiades xvii–xviii, 17–19, 31–4, 37, 38–9, 46, 49, 91, 96–7; Alexander xvii; Antony 31–2; Aristides xviii, 46; Lysander xviii, 91; Nicias xvii–xviii, 46; Pericles xviii; Pseudo-Plutarch, Lives of the Ten Orators 102; Solon 3
Potidaean campaign 24–7
Propontis (Sea of Marmara) 87
Pulytion 19, 58–9
Pylos 29, 39, 43, 86

Quadruple Alliance see Argive Alliance

Rhegion 53, 118n4

Salaminia 64–5
Samos 74, 76–80, 82, 88

Sardis 83, 90
Segesta 54–7, 62
Selymbria 86, 87, 88
Sestus 82, 83–4, 94, 95
Shakespeare, William xiv, 111n37
Sicily 41, 45, 53–8, 62–4, 68, 69
Socrates xiv, 1, 14, 19, 30, 33, 57,
    101; and Alcibiades 20–3;
    Aristophanes' caricature of 23;
    on Potidaean campaign 25–7
Solon 3, 100
Sophocles (general) 53–4
Sophocles (playwright) 1, 9
Sparta 50, 95; Alcibiades in 65–8;
    in Archidamian war 27–30,
    34–5; and battle of Aegospotami
    94–7; and battle of Mantinea
    44–5; envoys to Athens after
    battle of Cyzicus 86; envoys
    to Athens in 420 37–40; in
    Hellespontine war 82–8;
    problems after peace of Nicias
    36–7
Sphacteria 29, 34
Syracuse 53–4, 55, 56, 57, 64, 65,
    66

Teisias 51
Teucrus 59
Theagenes 2
Themistocles xix, 14, 53, 65, 97,
    117n1

Theopompus 45
Theramenes 80, 81, 84–5
Therimenes 70
Thessaly 67
Thirty Tyrants of Athens, the
    95–6, 98
Thracian Chersonese 84, 93, 95
Thrasybulus (general) 80, 82, 84–5
Thrasybulus (soldier) 93
Thrasyllus 82, 86–7, 88–9
Thucydides xiv–xvi, xx, 1, 7, 10,
    12, 13–15, 23, 35, 66, 89, 123n4;
    Archidamian war 27–30; coup of
    the Four Hundred 72–80;
    Melian Dialogue 49–50; peace
    of Nicias 36–45; Potidaean
    compaign 24–7; revolt of
    Athens' allies 69–72; Sicilian
    expedition 53–65
Timaea 67–8
Timandra 97
Timon 31–2
Tissaphernes 69–72, 75, 77–9, 82,
    90, 95, 126n59

Xenophon xvi–xvii, 1, 15, 22–3,
    83, 89, 91, 95; account of the
    battle of Cyzicus 84–6, 127n82,
    128n83; account of the battle of
    Notium 92–3

Zopyrus 18